LITERACY CIRCLES

A READY...SET...TEACH LITERATURE CIRCLE PROGRAM

for the CONTENT AREAS GRADES 6 - 12

Everything you need:
step-by-step procedures,
ready to use worksheets, & assessments

Written & Published by:
Sandra Rudolph & Helen Thompson:
The Reading Buddies

readingbuddies09@yahoo.com
1st Edition ~ Copyright 2009

MW01608938

LITERATURE CIRCLES:
**A READY...SET...TEACH LITERATURE CIRCLE PROGRAM
FOR THE CONTENT AREAS
GRADES 6-12**

1st Edition ~ The Reading Buddies © 2009

We encourage any questions, comments, or feedback regarding the use of this book.

Please send inquiries to <u>readingbuddies09@yahoo.com</u>

TABLE of CONTENTS

TABLE of CONTENTS Continued

ABOUT US: THE READING BUDDIES

<u>How it all began</u>: Helen Thompson & Sandy Rudolph's friendship began 'budding' when they were teaching at the same elementary school in Cape Coral, Florida, in 1996. One day they realized that their children were friends & they actually lived around the corner & down the street from each other! They soon discovered that their "motherly idiosyncrasies" were so alike it was scary! They remained friends even though their teaching paths took different directions for a few years. Then Helen coerced Sandy to teach reading with her in middle school. That's when they realized that their "teaching idiosyncrasies" or should we say 'styles' were so alike, it, too, was scary! They worked and planned together daily to develop effective ways to reinforce reading skills and instill a lifelong enjoyment of reading. As they explored ideas & taught Literature Circles they just couldn't find the right approach or materials to meet their middle school students' needs. They did not find "ready to teach" LITERATURE CIRCLE resources designed for middle school use so they created their own. The many, many hours spent researching, creating & revising their ideas, & adapting lesson plans led to the creation of this book. They have many ideas in the hopper, but started with one that would make an impact on reading comprehension. Their Literature Circle Program is intended to be user friendly & ready for immediate classroom use not only by reading or language arts teachers but middle & high school content area teachers as well.

<u>A bit more about the Bloomin' Buds</u>: Helen & Sandy are currently teaching middle school developmental, advanced, and intensive reading in Lee County, Florida. They are both National Board Certified Teachers, have been honored numerous times as Golden Apple Teacher Finalists in Lee County, Florida, as well as being recognized as Teacher of the Year.

Sandy's undergraduate work was completed at Michigan State University where she also completed a Master's Degree in Reading. Her love of teaching is reflected in 39 years of teaching experience ranging from grades 2-8 as well as developing and teaching a high school remedial reading program.

Helen is a graduate of Mansfield University in Pennsylvania. She has earned her Reading, Language Arts, and ESOL (English for Speakers of Other Languages) Endorsements. Her desire to touch children's lives over the past 13 years ranges from teaching grades 1, 2, & 4 as well as 6-7th grade language arts & 8th grade reading.

As their friendship & teaching relationship continued to grow, they jokingly referred to each other as "my reading buddy", which became "bud" or "buddy", so, what better name for their business partnership than "The Reading Buddies"!

ACKNOWLEDGEMENTS

Creating our own business "The Reading Buddies" has been a work in progress for several years. We have spent many long days, evenings, and weekends to make this endeavor a reality. Over the years we have worked diligently to create a "Ready, Set, Teach" Literature Circle Program for middle and high school educators in reading, language arts, and other content areas of the curriculum. We must thank those who provided invaluable support.

Our husbands (Ken & David), not only encouraged us but also tolerated the late evenings at school, working at home on this project, and took care of dinner on so many occasions. Our children, Jessie, Lindsey, Ben, Jessica, & daughter-in-law Amanda, were our best cheerleaders as they proudly provided their support and were eager to listen to our progress. Our sons-in-law (Justin & Steven) were our technological mentors as we picked their brains for advice. We are so grateful for our amazing families.

Many thanks are extended to all our friends and colleagues that we have had the privilege of working with over the years. Their confidence in our abilities encouraged us to pursue this dream.

We must acknowledge our students at Gulf Middle School and Challenger Middle School in Cape Coral, Florida. They were instrumental in "tweaking" our Literature Circle Program. Their positive reaction to literature circles inspired us. They offered remarkable feedback. The students' achievement & enjoyment of reading made it all worthwhile.

Sandra & Helen

OVERVIEW of LITERATURE CIRCLES

An INTRODUCTION to READY…SET…TEACH LITERATURE CIRCLES

Our program provides an opportunity for all students to implement effective reading strategies that ensure comprehension and retention of information read in novels or text book materials. The organization of our program enables all students an equal access to the learning process in a safe environment that lends itself to reading success. A spirit of enjoyment and engagement pervades the room with students on task. Class or group discussions are open conversations about the material being read encouraging both personal connections and open-ended questions. Our program is effective in content area classrooms as well as language arts, and reading classes.

Circles provide a cooperative learning experience in which students collaborate to better understand the material. It is student centered as they take responsibility for their own learning. **Literature Circles: A Ready…Set…Teach Literature Circle Program for the CONTENT AREAS Grades 6-12** was written to strategically reinforce and practice the essential skills that enhance comprehension for middle and high school students.

How do Literature Circles work?

Two of the most widely used processes are WHOLE or SMALL Group Literature Circles. The manner in which they are used can vary greatly from teacher to teacher. Our program is very detailed & provides you with all that you need to incorporate effective literature circles in your classroom. To ensure that students apply the essential reading skills correctly, it is imperative that the teacher be actively involved throughout the literature circle process. The teacher's role is explained throughout our program for both whole and small group circles.

To effectively practice reading skills, we have devised 10 different jobs that reinforce 21 different reading skills. The jobs establish a purpose for reading thus the students are actively involved in the reading process. Each day upon completion of whole or small group reading, students spend a short amount of time completing their jobs. Their work is shared with the class or group the next day before reading time is continued. There is a specific procedure that is easy to follow: sharing time, reading time, and time for independent completion of jobs. Students learn the process very quickly. Grades may be given for participation as well as quality and completion of written work. Organization is essential; we provide you with information on how to organize all the materials. A detailed explanation of whole & small group circles is provided, however the information below will provide an overview.

Overview of **WHOLE Group Circles**:
- The class reads the same book or textbook section together with the teacher.
- The book may be selected by the teacher or the class may vote on the book to be read from a selection of books available.
- The class meets on a regular schedule.
- It is best if students' desks/tables are arranged in a large circle (or square) so students can all see one another during discussions.

An INTRODUCTION to READY...SET...TEACH LITERATURE CIRCLES
continued

Overview of **WHOLE Group Circles** continued:

- The teacher models the role of facilitator with the intent of students learning the role. A gradual release of facilitative responsibilities is given to 1-2 students at a time.
- The teacher selects four or five jobs. Several students will have the same job based on their position in the circle. These students will keep their work in a Literature Circle folder. For example: with a class of 25, 5 jobs are selected & 5 students will have the same job. File folders are made for each group of 5 students to keep their work organized and make it easier for the teacher to evaluate their work.
- The jobs last for a 5-day cycle. On the 6th day, after sharing time, the jobs rotate around the circle and the new job sheets are distributed before reading begins.
- The class period is divided into: Sharing Time, Oral Reading Time, and Independent Work Time. This procedure continues until the book or textbook chapter is completed.
- End of the book Assessment ideas are provided for novels. If using a textbook, content area teachers' should use the tests that go along with their curriculum.

Overview of **SMALL Group Circles:**

- Small literature circle groups are formed based on students' choosing from a selection of available books or teacher's choice if using a textbook.
- Different groups may read different books.
- The groups meet on a regular schedule to read & discuss what they read. Each group's desks or tables should be placed together allowing as much space as possible between groups to lessen distractions.
- The teacher determines the skills to reinforce & selects 4-5 appropriate jobs.
- Of those 4-5 jobs students choose a job that will last for the 5-day cycle. No two persons in a group can have the same job at the same time nor can they do a job more than once.
- Each group has a Literature Circle folder for all of their work and charts. Specific information is given in the Small Group Section of this program.
- The jobs last for a 5-day cycle. On the 6th day, after sharing time, the members of the group choose a different job from those available and the cycle continues.
- The class period is divided so that each small group has a Sharing Time, Oral Reading Time, and Independent Work Time. This procedure continues until the book or textbook chapter is completed.
- Students facilitate their own groups rather than the teacher acting as the facilitator.
- The **TEACHER** is the **CHECKER**, monitoring participation as well as job quality and completion. Mini lessons may be incorporated into activities if needed. To ensure the success of literature circles, it is imperative that the teacher continuously moves from one group to another, listening, observing, and checking job sheets as the students read & discuss.
- End of the book Assessment ideas are provided. If the textbook is being used the content area teachers' should use the tests that go along with their curriculum.

Overview of Literature Circle JOB CHOICES

We've created 10 jobs that cover 21 reading skills. This overview gives a brief summary of each job explaining the skill(s), what may be done during reading time, after reading, and/or during sharing time the next day. You will select 4-5 jobs for a 5-day cycle. The student jobs can be used for both whole and small group literature circles. You may use this as a reference sheet with students.

*Didactic Detective: Skill: Cause & Effect. **You do NOT have your sheet out while reading.**

- **AFTER reading**: Determine **CAUSE (event)** and **EFFECT (Consequence-result) RELATIONSHIPS** in the selection EACH day.
- **SHARING TIME:** Discuss your cause/effect relationships with your group.

*Discussion Deliberator: Skill: Comprehension; Higher Level Thinking Skills. **You do NOT have your job sheet out while reading.**

- **DURING reading**: Encourage **CLARIFICATION** of information **as the GROUP READS.**
- **AFTER reading: Write 2 higher level thinking QUESTIONS** that would enhance comprehension of materials read or stimulate a thought provoking discussion. See Question Cue Card for ideas.
- **SHARING TIME**: You will ask these questions & encourage all members to contribute during your group discussion time. Then you will explain what the group discussed and give specific examples.

*Elemental Artist: Skill: Story Elements; Conflict/Resolution; Details; Main Idea; Plot Development. **You do NOT have your sheet out while reading.**

- **AFTER reading**: with a **simple drawing, depict an element** of the story from your reading <u>each day</u>: a Character; the Setting; a Problem; an Exciting Event; the Climax; or Resolution. Remember, you only have 5-8 minutes to complete your task.
- **SHARING TIME:** Share your drawing & explanation with your group.

*Lexicographer: Skill: Vocabulary Development; Dictionary/Thesaurus; Context Clues; Synonyms; Antonyms; Parts of Speech. **You USE your JOB SHEET while reading.**

- **DURING reading**: While you are reading with your group look for extended vocabulary words. If you find words that are challenging, thought provoking, puzzling or unfamiliar, write the PAGE & PARAGRAPH # and word on your job sheet.
- **AFTER reading:** Look words up in the DICTIONARY (use a computer dictionary/thesaurus, if available) and WRITE DOWN the DEFINITION that fits the context of your selection. Then, write the word's PART of SPEECH, a SYNONYM, & an ANTONYM.
- **SHARING TIME:** You will help members FIND the words in context and DISCUSS the meaning & other information, rather than merely reading from your sheet.

*Literary Enlightener: Skills: Figurative Language; Mood; Tone; Analyzing Text; Imagery. **You USE your JOB SHEET while reading. You will find thought provoking parts of the TEXT.**

- **DURING reading**: YOU **ONLY write the page & paragraph # on your job sheet** for the thought provoking words/text.
- **AFTER reading**: write the words from the text & explain why you selected this section.
- **SHARING TIME:** You will identify your selection & discuss your analysis.

Overview of Literature Circle JOB CHOICES continued

*Literary Locksmith: Skill: Character Development. **You do NOT have your sheet out while reading.**
- **AFTER reading**: select a character EACH day & "unlock" information about the character so that your group has a key to better understand this character.
- **SHARING TIME**: Discuss your character information with your group.

*Plot Predictor: Skill: Making Predictions; Drawing Conclusions; Inferences. **You do NOT have your job sheet out while reading.**
- **AFTER reading**: Make a prediction each day & confirm or un-confirm the previous day's prediction.
- **SHARING TIME**: Discuss your chart information with your group.

*Story Cartographer: Skill: Story Elements; Plot Development; Main Idea; Details. This job can be done **on a daily basis** with the understanding that all elements may not be evident in the daily readings, especially solution/outcomes. However, you may prefer to use the **STORY CARTOGRAPHER~END of the BOOK ASSESSMENT.** See Assessment section for more information.
- **AFTER reading**: Complete the story map each day based on what you read. You may not be able to complete the Solution/Outcome section daily.
- **SHARING TIME**: Discuss the information on your map with your group.

*Story Recapitulator: Skill: Comprehension; Main Idea; Details; Summarizing Key Events. **You do NOT have your sheet out while reading.**
- **AFTER reading**: It is your responsibility to write a brief **SUMMARY** (recap) of what the group read **TODAY**. Your summary should focus on the highlights or important parts of what you read, including the key events.
- **SHARING TIME**: Share your summary (recap) as a review of what you read.

*Text Connector: Skill: Text Connections. **You do NOT have your sheet out while reading.**
- **AFTER reading**: Write one interesting connection between your reading & the world beyond the book: Text to **Self**; Text to **World**; Text to **Text.**
- **SHARING TIME**: You will explain your personal connection with your group.

ADDITIONAL INFORMATION:
  - ➢ Remember, you SELECT the JOBS based on the SKILLS that you want to reinforce during the Literature Circle Time.
  - ➢ Not all jobs are used within a 5-day cycle. Select 4-5 jobs.
  - ➢ It is wise to always have a RECAPITULATOR so that a SUMMARY is given each day during sharing time.
  - ➢ We've created a recommended ORDER of DISCUSSION for the jobs primarily based on a logical order with consideration to the importance of the skill.
  - ➢ The following page is a CROSS REFERENCE of READING SKILLS and JOBS. The jobs are LISTED IN THE RECOMMENDED ORDER OF DISCUSSION mentioned above.

CROSS REFERENCE of READING SKILLS and JOBS

JOBS

Jobs	Analyzing Words in Text	Author's Purpose & Point of View	Cause & Effect	Character Development	Compare & Contrast	Conflict & Conflict Resolution	Context Clues	Details	Drawing Conclusions	Figurative Language	Main Idea	Mood	Personal Connections Text to: Self, World, Text	Plot Development	Predictions	Reference Skills	Summarizing	Story Elements	Tone and/or Descriptive Language	Vocabulary Development
Story Recapitulator								X			X						X			
Discussion Deliberator		X	X		X	X			X	X	X	X		X	X			X	X	
Story Cartographer					X		X				X			X				X		
Literary Locksmith				X																
Lexicographer	X						X									X				X
Literary Enlightener	X									X		X							X	
Didactic Detective		X																		
Elemental Artist					X		X				X			X				X		
Text Connector													X							
Plot Predictor									X						X					

READING SKILLS →

An X in the coordinates indicates the skill(s) practiced in each of the 10 jobs. This chart will assist you in selecting appropriate jobs to reinforce specific skills and better meet students' needs to enhance comprehension.

Jobs are listed in the recommended order of discussion.

Procedures for Students that Are Absent

It is important for students to complete any work they missed while absent. To help them catch up, this procedure worked best for us.

If a student is absent one day:
On the day of his/her return, it is important that the student remains in the circle during sharing time then moves to a quiet area to **read the pages he/she missed the day of the absence.** Pages read can be found on the Small Group Progress Sheet or from another student's job sheet. The student should **complete the job sheet section** for those pages. If there is time, he/she should begin the next section.

For homework, the student checks out the book to make up or finish the current day's reading & job sheet section. Thus, he/she will be in synch with the group & ready to share the next day. If the work is not made up in a sufficient amount of time, the student gets a 0 for that section on the job sheet for each day that is missing. By allowing class time for make-up work it is a rarity to have a student not be in synch with his/her group within a short period of time.

How are books checked out?
To ensure that there is a book available for every student to read in class each day, it is necessary to have a separate set of "extra" books to be checked out to make up missed work. Establishing a container of extra copies for ABSENT BOOK CHECK OUT is essential. A photo example of a book check out container for small group circles can be found in the Appendix – Photo Gallery. In this picture, you will notice that there are multiple copies of each book being used by the small groups. You would also have a Book Check Out container if you were conducting a whole group literature circle. We have created a Book Check Out Sheet (template) for students to use when a book is checked out. It is located in the Appendix.

Due to multiple copies of 1 title available for check out, it is wise to put a code or number on the inside cover of the books to be sure that the correct book was returned to you. For example: CO-1 (Checked Out - Book 1), CO-2, etc. Then this code is written with the book title on the check out sheet. This may seem time consuming, but it isn't. It is worthwhile to be sure the correct books are checked out and returned, rather than someone attempting to return a book from those kept in the classroom. These books for check out should be in a separate area & all books should be checked out through the teacher. This process eliminated lost books.

If a student is absent for several days:
On the day of his/her return, the student should record all the dates and pages missed on each section of the job sheet. Missed work can be found on the Small Group Progress Sheet or from another student's job sheet. Because he/she is more than a day behind, it is not necessary to be with the group during sharing time. The student moves to a quiet area to read the **pages he/she missed starting from the beginning of the absences.** The student should **complete the job sheet section** for each group of pages missed.

For homework, the student checks out the book to continue to make up the reading & job sheet sections. Allow class time to expedite the completion of work so he/she will be able to rejoin the group in a timely fashion. If the student missed several days, establish a deadline to complete the make up work. If the work is not made up by the deadline, the student gets a 0 for each day that is missing on the job sheet.

GRADING: Absent students will earn a JOB QUALITY & COMPLETION grade based on the job sheet sections completed. However, they do not earn the 20 points for a PARTICIPATE & COOPERATE grade on any day absent. For example: 4 days present x 20 possible daily points = 80 total possible points. The grade is based on the # of points earned divided by 80. Let's say, the student earns 75 points of the 80 possible so, 75 divided by 80 = 94%. This is a fair and equitable means of grading. The student is not being penalized for being absent, but is held accountable for his/her participation and cooperation for the days he/she is in attendance.

LESSON PLANS ~ AN OVERVIEW

Every teacher or school has different formats that are used for writing and/or submitting lesson plans to their administrator. Included are 2 lesson plan options for using Literature Circles in your classroom.

Lesson Plan Option 1:

Lesson plans are written in a 1-page explanation of literature circle plans. There is a separate page for small and whole group literature circles.

Lesson Plan Option 2:

Lesson plans are written on a formatted page that includes Instructional Strategies. This is the weekly format that we use for our lesson plans. Our district requires the state standards, ESOL (English for Speakers of Other Languages) strategies, & ESE (Exceptional Student Education) Modifications in our lesson plans. The appropriate strategies are highlighted for each week's plans based on the job skills that are being reinforced. There is a separate page for small and whole group literature circles.

These options are located in both Literature Circle sections.

SUCCESS of the CIRCLE
GUIDELINES

WHY SHOULD I CREATE "SUCCESS of the CIRCLE" GUIDELINES?

Determining expectations for work habits and behavior choices during Literature Circles are imperative for a successful learning experience.

Some teachers may feel more comfortable creating their own expectations and sharing them with their students. However, we recommend that you involve students in the process. Helping to create the guidelines for success provides an opportunity for students to take ownership of the decisions. Contributing to and acceptance of the expectations empowers students; Therefore, they are more likely to comply with the expectations. If students waiver from the expectations, simply pointing to the chart will often automatically correct the behavior, eliminating the need for verbal correction.

HOW DO I INVOLVE STUDENTS IN DETERMINING EXPECTATIONS?

Option 1: The teacher leads a discussion on the importance of having guidelines during Literature Circles. Students brainstorm ideas together as a class.

Option 2: The teacher leads a discussion on the importance of having guidelines during Literature Circles. Using a co-operative learning strategy, divide the class into groups. Each group prepares a list of suggestions that they will share with the class.

- Regardless of which option you use, the ideas are recorded for all to see (on chart paper, an overhead, or on whiteboard, etc.). We recommend creating one for each class. Use a T Chart format with columns labeled acceptable and unacceptable.
- Some suggestions can be combined together. Ideas should be condensed into phrases.
- Ultimately it is best to have all + expectations. Discuss expectations on the "- Unacceptable" side and rewrite them in a positive manner. Instead of "Don't waste time when you come into class" write "Begin Circle promptly".
- When the ideas have all been recorded, review the list to see if any changes should be made.
- Now for the "empowering" step…it is important that you ask the class & yourself: "Can you (I) accept these expectations? In other words, "Is this something we can live with?" If not, then revise any guidelines so they can be accepted.
- Display each class' SUCCESS of the CIRCLE Chart

An example of a SUCCESS of the CIRCLE T-Chart and a Positive Expectation Chart are included in this section.

CCESS of the CIRCLE

PECTED	— UNACCEPTABLE
• Be polite/respectful	* Being rude/critical
• Take turns	* Interrupting
• Participate	* Private conversations
• On task	* Foolishness
• Focused	* Name calling
• Voice your opinion	* Off topic
• Disagree politely	* Laughing or being
• Be patient	disrespectful of
• Follow along in book	others' point of view
• Stay on TOPIC	
• Encourage others	
• Give Compliments	
• 1 speaker at a time	
• Ask relevant questions	
• Begin Circle Promptly	

Note: After brainstorming ideas on a T-chart, guide students to restate the negative comments in a positive way. These positive statements will be your draft to create a Success of the Circle Expectations Chart for all to accept, then post for each class. See page 12-b and photo example on Appendix page 78

Literature Circles: The Reading Buddies © 2009

SUCCESS of the CIRCLE

1. Participate actively
2. Pay attention
3. Work quietly
4. Follow along while reading
5. Share information
6. Be on task
7. Be respectful and kind
8. Listen
9. Voice your opinion
10. Disagree politely
11. Take turns
12. Begin work promptly

WHOLE GROUP LITERATURE CIRCLES

Process & Procedures for
ORGANIZING WHOLE GROUP LITERATURE CIRCLES

WHOLE GROUP Literature Circles are recommended to introduce students to Literature Circles. It is an effective way to "model" higher-level discussion questions, expected behaviors, as well as the different job responsibilities prior to using small group circles. Using the job sheets reinforces reading skills & enhances comprehension. Using a whole group circle early in the school year paves the way for cooperative groups and sets expectations that all students will be active participators in the learning process.

Step 1: Getting Started

1. The teacher may use a chapter or section of a **textbook**.
2. If a **literature book** is used, the **teacher** may determine the selection of the book:
   - ❑ To read a genre or a subject that students may not select themselves.
   - ❑ To complement a unit or theme being studied.
   - ❑ To correlate with topics being studied in other classes.
3. If a **literature book** is used, the **students** may determine the selection of the book.
   - ❑ Teacher presents creative short "Book Talks" of pre-selected books that are available as a class set.
   - ❑ Provide time for students to look at the book, read cover, & share interests.
   - ❑ Students vote on their FIRST choice from the book talks.
   - ❑ The top 3 books from this vote are briefly reviewed.
   - ❑ The class votes on these 3 books. The winner is the book that's read as a class.
3. Teacher determines the number of JOBS (skills) to be reinforced depending on the size and needs of the class. Maximum recommended number is 4-5 jobs.
   - ❑ Multiple students may have the SAME JOB or the whole group could work on 1 job.
   - ❑ Make copies of the job sheets to be used.

Step 2: Room Setup & Storage of Materials

1. Teacher
   - ❑ Determines room arrangement for interactive discussions (preferably in a circle or U shape, if possible).
   - ❑ Teacher has dictionaries & thesauruses readily available (1 per group) or access to Internet reference sources for the Lexicographer's job.
   - ❑ Assign the jobs by the seating arrangement rather than having students select a job as they do in small literature circles. Students with the same job should be sitting next to one another. This is a time saver & helps with organizing materials in the groups' literature circle folders. This is an efficient way to provide assistance if they are having any difficulty with the job (skill). It allows you to merely rotate the jobs around the circle every 5 days.
2. Teacher has all materials ready for WHOLE Group Literature Circle:
   - ❑ Multiple copies of chosen book; 1 per student is best.
   - ❑ Student JOB sheets organized in a folder for each JOB GROUP. You can number the groups or use table #s.
   - ❑ "CHECKER'S DAILY & 5-Day Cycle REPORT...TEACHER" sheet.
   - ❑ Whole Group Progress Sheet

Step-by-Step Directions for
CONDUCTING WHOLE Group Literature Circle Meetings Steps 1-3

STEP 1: INTRODUCTION

1. Teacher showing the job sheets, briefly discusses jobs (skills) & responsibilities of literature circles from "Overview of Literature Circle Job Choices".
2. Determine Expectations & Behavior during Literature Circles.
   - ❑ Teacher may lead a discussion on expectations & behavior during Literature Circles.
   - ❑ Co-operative Activity: groups of students discuss suggestions & share with the class. See "Success of the Circle Guidelines".
   - ❑ Use suggestions to create a T-chart for "Success of the Circle" expectations. Refer to the posted chart(s) as needed.
3. Pass "CHECKER'S DAILY & 5-Day Cycle REPORT…TEACHER" sheet around the circle having students write their name & job. This will save you time. Having the names in order around the circle expedites the monitoring of participation & engagement and recording points for daily jobs during Sharing Time.
4. Distribute ready-made folders to each job group.
   - ❑ Students write their names on new job sheets.
   - ❑ Put job sheets in the "group" folder.
   - ❑ Explain where the group's folder will be stored at the end of class.

Step 2: FIRST WHOLE GROUP Literature Circle Meeting:

1. Upon entering, each student obtains a copy of the book. Passing them out as they enter is advised.
2. Class begins reading taking turns reading the text aloud. It's recommended that a student reads at least 1-2 pages rather than breaking the text into smaller segments. Switching readers too often will affect comprehension & fluency.
3. Discuss or clarify text as you read.
4. **LAST 5-8 MINUTES** of class: (Teacher sets timer.)
   - ❑ Distribute Group Folders so students have their individual jobs sheets.
   - ❑ Students complete their jobs quietly on their individual job sheets.
   - ❑ Teacher records DATE & PAGES READ on the WHOLE GROUP PROGRESS Sheet.
   - ❑ Students put all job sheets in their group's Literature Circle folder.
   - ❑ Return FOLDERS to the correct storage area.
   - ❑ Collect BOOKS & store in designated place. To avoid losing books collect them as students exit.

STEP 3: SUBSEQUENT DAILY PROCEDURES for WHOLE GROUP Meetings:

1. Teacher passes out books as students enter.
2. The first to enter from each group gets the Group's File Folder & distributes job sheets to members of the group.
3. **FIRST 10-12 Minutes** of class **SHARING TIME**: (Teacher sets timer.)
   - ❑ Due to time restraints, one member of EACH group shares his/her job with the class.
   - ❑ Students should be patient; not everyone shares each day. Use the Whole Group Checker sheet 'Job Quality & Completion' column to record a grade as a student shares his/her job. This allows you to keep track of who has shared, who needs to share, & who was absent.
   - ❑ Be sure everyone has a chance to participate within the 5-day cycle.

Step-by-Step Directions
for
CONDUCTING WHOLE Group Literature Circle Meetings Steps 4-5

4. Begin **READING**: (Set timer to allow 5-8 minutes for jobs at the end of class.)
   - Initially the teacher models the facilitator's role leading the circle & discussion. Eventually designate a student to be the facilitator after you have modeled for them.
   - As the class reads, the teacher monitors student participation & engagement using the "CHECKER'S DAILY & 5-Day Cycle REPORT…TEACHER" sheet.

5. **Last 5-8 minutes of class:**
   - Students do jobs quietly and independently.
   - Clean up work area returning file folders to designated container.
   - Collect books as students exit.

TEACHER GRADES JOB SHEETS:

To maximize learning & job quality we recommend that you monitor students' jobs offering feedback regularly to enhance students' performance on job sheets.

> A grade may be given based on the job quality the day students **share** with the group.

> You may choose to grade each section of the job sheet for a weekly grade based on 20 points per day.

> Write grade(s) earned on the "CHECKER'S DAILY & 5-Day Cycle REPORT…TEACHER" sheet.

On the 6th or possibly the 11thday:

- Students share jobs completed the previous day. This should be the LAST section of their 5-day cycle job sheet.
- The group's COMPLETED JOB SHEETS are **stapled together** & **remain** in the group's literature circle folder.
- **NEW JOBS** are **rotated clockwise** around the circle.
   - ✓ Distribute new job sheets to each group.
   - ✓ Each student writes name & book title on his/her job sheet. Pass a new "CHECKER'S DAILY & 5 Day Cycle REPORT…TEACHER" sheet around the circle having students write their name & new job. This will save you time. Having the names in order around the circle expedites the monitoring of participation & engagement and recording points for daily jobs.
   - ✓ Group resumes reading their book.

REPEAT DAILY PROCEDURES until the book or textbook chapter is finished.

END of BOOK ASSESSMENT: A variety of assessment options are provided. If the textbook is being used content area teachers' should use the tests that go along with their curriculum.

OPTION 1: LESSON PLANS for WHOLE GROUP LITERATURE CIRCLES

School: _____ Class: _____

Teacher: _____ Week of: _____

GOAL: All students will implement effective reading strategies that ensure comprehension and retention of information read in novels or textbook materials.

STUDENT OBJECTIVES: Students will:
1. Discuss, define, & explore unfamiliar words.
2. Draw conclusions and predict text events using previous knowledge & details in the text.
3. Use evidence in the text to verify predictions.
4. Ask relevant, focused, higher level questions to check for comprehension and clarify any misconceptions.
5. Respond to questions & discussion with relevant & focused comments.
6. Paraphrase & summarize information from the text.
7. Identify & analyze literary elements.

Plans for WHOLE GROUP Literature Circle:
Students participate in a whole group Literature Circle based on a class vote of a pre-selected group of books or teacher's decision. Textbook sections can also be used in a whole group circle. Each student has a job (skill) that is changed at the end of the 5-day cycle. Three to five students may do the same job. See specific processes & procedures in teacher's folder for organization & discussions prior to beginning the whole group literature circle.

FIRST & SUBSEQUENT DAYS of the CIRCLE:
See specific procedures in teacher's folder.

On the 6th (&11th day), after sharing time: NEW jobs will be rotated & assigned for the next 5-day cycle. NEW JOB SHEETS are distributed before beginning the day's reading so students are aware of their new responsibilities.

JOBS/SKILLS: (Insert jobs/skills to be practiced.)

DAILY PROCEDURES:
Teacher greets students at the door. (If novel is being used, hand them a copy of the book. Textbooks should be at work area.). The first to **enter** from their group should get the group's folder. Within 2 minutes, students should be seated at their designated seating area with their job sheet.

During **sharing time**, 1 student from each skill group shares each day. All skills should be shared within 10-12 minutes. Be sure each student has shared by the end of the 5-day cycle.

Then the students take turns **reading** aloud.

During the last 5-8 minutes of class, students do their **jobs** quietly and independently. Job sheets are returned to group's folder & put away during clean up. Novels are collected as students exit.

TEACHER'S DAILY ASSESSMENT: As the students read aloud, the teacher monitors student participation & engagement using "Whole Group Checker's Daily & 5-Day Cycle Report…TEACHER" sheet. Two grades per student may be given based on daily participation and cooperation & the quality and completion of his/her job within the 5-day cycle. See **"Checker's Daily and 5-Day Cycle Report…Teacher"** for details on grading.

END of BOOK ASSESSMENTS: A variety of assessment options are available. If a textbook is being used, content area teachers should use the test that coincides with the curriculum.

TEACHER: _____

Class: _____

20___ - 20___

Week of: _____

Sunshine State Standards	**Instructional Strategies**

Sunshine State Standards

LA.A. 1.3.1 Predictions
LA.A. 1.3.2 Conclusions & Inferences
LA.A. 1.3.3 Vocabulary/Words in Context
LA.A 1.3.4 Comprehension
LA.A. 2.3.1 Main Idea & Details
LA.A. 2.3.2 Author's Purpose/Point of View
LA.A. 2.3.5 Locates/Organizes Information
LA.A.2.3.6 Uses Reference Materials
LA.A 2.3.7 Compare/ Contrast
LA.A.2.3.8 Fact Opinion, Weak/Strong
              Arguments
LA.C. 1.3.2 Listens to readings
LA.C. 1.3.4 Summarizing/Paraphrasing
LA.D.1.3.4 Poetry Techniques
LA.D.1.3.5 Identifies Common Themes in
              Literature
LA.E.1.3.2 Plot/Setting/Conflict Resolution
LA.E.1.3.3 Figurative Language
LA.E.2.2.1 Cause & Effect
LA.E. 2.3.1 Character Development
LA.E. 2.3.3 Responses to text
LA.E.2.3.7 Reading for personal pleasure

ESOL Strategies

Activate Background
  Knowledge
Adult/Peer Tutor
Audio/Visual
Cooperative Learning
Direct Instruction
Graphic Organizers
Computer-Technology
Manipulatives
Realia
Self/Peer Assessment
Vocab. Development

ESE MODIFICATIONS

Alternate Evaluation
Extra Time
Flexible Scheduling
Hardcopy of Notes
Key Points
Manipulatives
Modify Assessments
Organizational
  Skills/Strategies
Peer Tutor
Preferential Seating
Proximity Control
Redirection
Test Preview
Use of computer proj.
Use of Planner
Wait Time
Graphic Organizers
Co-operative Groups

MEETINGS:

Mon:

Tues

Wed:

Thur:

Fri:

HOMEWORK:

DISMISSAL DUTY:

Instructional Strategies

Plans for WHOLE GROUP Literature Circle
Students participate in a WHOLE group Literature Circle based upon a class vote from a pre-selected group of books, teacher decision, or textbook section. Each student has a job that is changed at the end of the 5-day cycle. Three to five students do the same job. See specific processes & procedures in teacher's folder prior to beginning the Circle.

GOAL: All students will implement effective reading strategies that ensure comprehension and retention of information read in novels or textbook materials.
STUDENT OBJECTIVES: Students will:
1. Discuss, define, & explore unfamiliar words.
2. Draw conclusions & predict events using previous knowledge & details from the text.
3. Use evidence in the text to verify predictions.
4. Ask relevant, focused, & higher level questions to check for comprehension and clarify any misconceptions.
5. Respond to questions & discussions with relevant & focused comments.
6. Paraphrase & summarize information from the text.
7. Identify & analyze literary elements in the text.
FIRST & SUBSEQUENT DAYS of the Circle: See specific procedures in teacher's folder.
On the 6th (&11th day), after sharing time: NEW jobs will be rotated & assigned for the next 5-day cycle. NEW JOB SHEETS are distributed before beginning the day's reading so students are aware of their new responsibilities.
JOBS/SKILLS: (Insert jobs/skills to be practiced.)

DAILY PROCEDURES: Teacher greets students at the door handing them a copy of the book. The first to enter from their group should get the group's folder. Within 2 minutes, students should be seated at their designated seats with their job sheet. The teacher calls on a student from each group for Sharing Time (discussions of jobs). Students share, as much as possible, in approximately 10-12 minutes. Then the students take turns reading aloud. During the last 5-8 minutes of class, students do their jobs quietly and independently. Job sheets are returned to group's folder & put away during clean up. Teacher collects books as students exit. If textbooks are used, they remain at desks.
TEACHER DAILY ASSESSMENT: As the students read aloud, the teacher monitors student participation & engagement using "Checker's Daily & 5-Day Cycle Report...TEACHER". Two grades per student may be given based on daily participation and cooperation & the quality and completion of his/her job. See "Checker's Daily and 5-Day Report...Teacher" for details on grading.
OTHER ASSESSMENTS: A variety of assessment options are available. If a textbook is being used, content area teachers should use the test that coincides with the curriculum.

Option 2: Lesson Plans formatted with FL Standards & Strategies (WHOLE Group)

WHOLE GROUP RECORD SHEET of JOBS   Option 1

JOBS

Story Recapitulator																			
Discussion Deliberator																			
Story Cartographer																			
Literary Locksmith																			
Lexicographer																			
Literary Enlightener																			
Didactic Detective																			
Elemental Artist																			
Text Connector																			
Plot Predictor																			
→ WHOLE GROUP LITERATURE CIRCLE CLASS LIST																			

**Check off students' jobs each 5 - Day Cycle
to keep track of JOB EXPERIENCES.
Jobs are listed in recommended order of discussion.**

WHOLE GROUP RECORD of JOBS   Option 2

- Each student writes his/her name as sheet circulates clockwise around the circle.
- Jobs will be **changed every 5 days.**
- At the **beginning of a NEW CYCLE**, each student writes the NAME of his/her **New Job**
- **No member should have the same job twice.**

Student's Name:	Dates of Job Cycles _____ to _____	Dates of Job Cycles _____ to _____	Dates of Job Cycles _____ to _____

WHOLE GROUP PROGRESS SHEET
LITERATURE CIRCLE
This sheet is COMPLETED <u>EACH</u> DAY

Title of Book: _____

DATE CLASS STARTED the BOOK: _____

EACH DAY, COMPLETE the READING Information below
to indicate class progress while reading this book.

Date		Read From Page		To	
Date		Read From Page		To	
Date		Read From Page		To	
Date		Read From Page		To	
Date		Read From Page		To	
Date		Read From Page		To	
Date		Read From Page		To	
Date		Read From Page		To	
Date		Read From Page		To	
Date		Read From Page		To	
Date		Read From Page		To	
Date		Read From Page		To	
Date		Read From Page		To	
Date		Read From Page		To	
Date		Read From Page		To	
Date		Read From Page		To	
Date		Read From Page		To	
Date		Read From Page		To	
Date		Read From Page		To	
Date		Read From Page		To	
Date		Read From Page		To	

TEACHER'S ROLE: <u>CHECKER ~ WHOLE GROUP</u> Literature Circles

Prior to reading on the first day of the Literature Circle, circulate the **"Whole Group Checker's Daily & 5-Day Cycle Report...Teacher"** sheet clockwise around the circle starting with the first group of students with the same job. Each student fills in his/her name & the job he/she has for the 5-day cycle. This saves you time & has all the names in order around the circle expediting any record keeping on this grading sheet. A new sheet is completed when you start a new 5-day cycle. The jobs will rotate & you'll have a new grading sheet. A template of this record sheet is found on the next page.

DURING WHOLE group reading time, the TEACHER:
- Sits in the circle with the class following along as students are reading aloud.
- Models the facilitator's role so that students can assume the role as facilitator when ready. The facilitator:
  - o Determines the process for selecting the next reader.
  - o Asks higher level thinking questions to enhance comprehension or clarify any difficult passages.
  - o Keeps track of time using a timer.
- Monitors students' participation and engagement using the "Whole Group Checker's Daily & 5-Day Cycle Report...Teacher".
  - o This is your record sheet for determining a Participation & Cooperation grade at the end of the 5-day cycle. If any student is off task, put a minus - under Participate/Cooperate & encourage student(s) to refocus. A maximum of 20 points is earned each day. Points are deducted from 100 for each minus at the end of the 5-day cycle.
  - o Should read to model expression & fluency.

DURING SHARING TIME at the beginning of class, the TEACHER:
- Calls upon 1 member of each JOB GROUP to share. There is not enough time for every student to share each day.
- Evaluates the student's JOB based on what is shared & records the number of points received in the appropriate box under JOB QUALITY & COMPLETION. You may want to look at the job sheet while the student is sharing to help determine points received. 20 points are earned per day.
- On the record sheet, each box is 1 day in the 5-day cycle. Writing the number of points earned from sharing on a particular day helps you to keep track of who has shared in each job group so that everyone is called upon by the end of the week.
- If you choose, this 1 sharing grade can be the student's Job Quality & Completion grade for the week...but be sure that work is **accurately** completed on the **rest of the sheet**.
- If you prefer, you can grade the other sections of the job sheet at another time during the 5-day cycle (the sooner the better) & write the scores on your record sheet & the student's job sheet. This is more time consuming, but provides more feedback to students and encourages their best effort. If a student is having difficulty with the job sheet or understanding the skill, staple a **<u>"SEE ME before completing today's section of your job sheet"</u>** note on the student's paper. Clarify any misconceptions immediately. A template   for these SEE ME notes is located in the Appendix.

WHILE STUDENTS ARE DOING JOBS INDEPENDENTLY the TEACHER:

- Provides assistance if needed.
- May choose to correct previously done sections of job sheets as students are working.

END of the 5-DAY CYCLE: Using information from "CHECKER'S DAILY & 5-DAY CYCLE REPORT...TEACHER", the teacher determines **2 grades per week** based on:

- **Participation/cooperation points**
    - 100-5 (or 10) for each minus = participation grade. You can determine your own value for each minus - . (Five or ten points are recommended.)

- **Job quality/completion points**
    - If you check the entire job sheet, add up daily points/day on weekly job sheet to determine grade.
      20 points per day = 100 per week, so total points = % grade.
    - If you take a grade only on the day a student has shared with the group then compute your grade based on the quality of work for that day using either 20 points or 100 points. This is entirely your decision.

Enjoy working with students in the circle.
Encourage thought provoking discussions.
Praise students often.
Have high expectations for work habits & behavior.

Students will rise to the occasion!

WHOLE GROUP CHECKER'S DAILY & 5-DAY CYCLE REPORT...TEACHER

Teacher:
evaluates **PARTICIPATION/COOPERATION** daily. A specific number of points is deducted for each minus.
Monitors &/or corrects sheets for **JOB QUALITY & COMPLETION**.
Grades are given for **Participation/Cooperation** and **Job Quality/Completion** at the end of the 5-Day Cycle.

BOOK: _____ Dates of 5-Day Cycle_____

Author: _____

STUDENTS' NAMES **CLOCKWISE** AROUND the CIRCLE	**YOUR JOB THIS WEEK**	**PARTICIPATE & COOPERATE**					**JOB QUALITY & COMPLETION**					**PARTICIPATE COOPERATE 5-Day Cycle GRADE**	**JOB 5-Day Cycle GRADE**

Process & Procedures for
ORGANIZING SMALL GROUP LITERATURE CIRCLES Steps 1-3

Step 1: Getting Started

1. Teacher presents short "Book Talks" (reviews) of pre-selected books that are available in multiple copies (at least 6-7 copies).

2. Students write their TOP 3 choices of books presented by the teacher.

3. Teacher collects choices. Then makes a list of books & writes names of students under their FIRST choice. See **"Small Group Literature Circle~ Organizational Worksheet"** for specifics.

Step 2: Preparation of Materials

1. Teacher has all needed materials **READY for distribution** to groups.

   - ❏ Multiple copies of book. (1 title per container) to be used by different classes with a "place" where they will be picked up & returned to each day.

   - ❏ LABEL each container with the Book Title so all books are returned to the correct place.

   - ❏ Make a File Folder for each group. On the inside of the folder staple:

     - ✓ Progress Sheet & Record of Weekly Job Assignments, These can be run back to back, & stapled to right side of Literature Circle Folder.

     - ✓ "Checker's Daily and 5-Day Cycle Report...TEACHER" stapled to left side of folder (for teacher's daily/5-day evaluation).

   - ❏ Label a **"Literature Circle FOLDERS"** container for each class.
   - ❏ Make copies of job (skill) sheets that will be used.

Step 3:   Room Setup & Storage of Materials

1. Teacher arranges the room according to #s in the literature circle groups based upon book choice. Leave as much space as possible between groups.

2. Teacher has dictionaries & thesauruses readily available (1 per group) or access to Internet reference sources for the Lexicographer's job.

3. Designate a place for the book containers and a place for file folders containers.

4. Organize job sheets that are being used on a table or in file folders for students to access easily each 5-day cycle as jobs are chosen.

Process & Procedures for
ORGANIZING SMALL GROUP LITERATURE CIRCLES Step 4

Step 4: Introduction

1. **Teacher shows** students where:
   - Books are stored (labeled containers for each book).

   - File folders are kept. (Recommend 1 container per class period).

2. **Teacher MODELS** then has a group demonstrate how students enter class, pick up materials quietly, and begin their literature circle. Groups do not wait for teacher or other groups. They start as soon as all are present.

3. **Teacher discusses** jobs & responsibilities of literature circles from the Overview handout. Due to the large number of jobs available, you can select the skills (jobs) that you want to concentrate on, thus limiting the number of choices. You can add new choices the 2nd week if you choose.

4. **Students LABEL** file folders for each group:
   - Write BOOK TITLE & Period number on the tab.

   - Then a list of group members is written on the front of the folder.

   - Students will keep their job sheet in the Literature Circle File Folder. (At the end of the 5-day cycle, staple the job sheets & keep them in the folder).

5. **Groups decide** which JOB each student will have for the 5-day cycle. There is no duplication of a job within the group. (Depending on the size of the group, all jobs may not be assigned).

6. **Students get** their job assignment sheet.
   - Each student writes his/her name & book title on job sheet.

   - Be sure students understand that a NEW SECTION of the sheet is used EACH DAY for a total of 5 days.

   - A group member completes the TOP portion of the "Small Group Progress Sheet" that is stapled to the inside of the folder.

   - Students complete the first 2 columns of the RECORD of 5-Day JOB ASSIGNMENTS that is stapled in their group's folder.

7. **Determine Expectations & Behavior** during Literature Circles
   - Teacher may lead a discussion on expectations & have suggestions recorded.
   - Co-operative Activity: groups of students discuss suggestions & then share with the group.
   - Use suggestions to create a T-chart for "Success of the Circle" Expectations. Refer to the posted chart(s) as needed.

Step-by-Step Directions
for
ONDUCTING Small Group Literature Circle Meetings
Step 1

Step 1: FIRST SMALL GROUP Literature Circle Meeting:

1. **Explain** to students that:

   ❑ Folders are left open on the center of the table so teacher can note any + or – for participation and points after correcting job sheets.

   ❑ Each group member has a copy of the book & the correct job sheet.

   ❑ Job sheets are kept UNDER the folder unless the job sheet specifies that it be used during reading.

2. Groups **begin reading** taking turns reading the text aloud. It's recommended that a student read at least 1-2 pages rather than breaking the text into smaller segments. Switching readers too often will affect comprehension & fluency.

3. Students will discuss or clarify text as they read.

4. Students **read** until teacher announces the end of reading time.

5. **LAST 10 MINUTES** of class: (Set timer to ring when 10 minutes are left)

   ❑ Students complete their jobs quietly on their individual job sheets.

   ❑ A designated group member is selected to record DATE & PAGES READ for each day on the PROGRESS SHEET in the file folder.

   ❑ PUT all JOB SHEETS in the group's Literature Circle folder.

   ❑ Put folders in the class' container.

   ❑ Return books to the correct storage area.

Step-by-Step Directions
for
CONDUCTING SMALL Group Literature Circle Meetings Steps 2-3

Step 2: Subsequent Literature Circle Meetings:

1. Students enter, get materials for their group, and start within 1-2 minutes.

2. **FIRST 5 - 8 Minutes** of class: (Teacher sets timer)

   ❑ Each person shares his/her job that was completed the previous day.

   ❑ Students are polite and attentive during sharing.

   ❑ Folder is left open on the center of the table.

   ❑ After sharing, job sheets are kept under the folder unless it is specified that the job sheet be used DURING READING.

3. **Next 20 minutes** (time may vary depending on the length of your class period):

   ❑ Groups **read** taking turns reading the text aloud.

   ❑ Teacher circulates around the room monitoring groups and checking job sheets for quality & completion of work.

4. **Last 8-10 minutes** of class:

   ❑ Students complete their jobs quietly on their individual job sheets.

   ❑ A designated group member is selected to record DATE & PAGES READ for each day on the PROGRESS SHEET in the file folder.

   ❑ PUT all JOB SHEETS in the group's Literature Circle folder.

   ❑ Put folders in the class' container.

   ❑ Return books to the correct storage area.

5. REPEAT DAILY procedures until book or textbook chapter is finished.

Step 3: END of BOOK ASSESSMENT: A variety of assessment options are provided. If the textbook is being used content area teachers' should use the tests that coincide with the curriculum.

Note: Remember to have students switch jobs at the end of each 5-day cycle.

OPTION 1: LESSON PLANS for SMALL GROUP LITERATURE CIRCLES

School: _____

Teacher: _____   Week of: _____

GOAL: All students will implement effective reading strategies that ensure comprehension and retention of information read in novels or textbook materials.

STUDENT OBJECTIVES: Students will:
1. Discuss, define, & explore unfamiliar words.
2. Draw conclusions and predict text events using previous knowledge & details in the text.
3. Use evidence in the text to verify predictions.
4. Ask relevant, focused, higher level questions to check for comprehension and clarify any misconceptions.
5. Respond to questions & discussion with relevant & focused comments.
6. Paraphrase & summarize information from the text.
7. Identify & analyze literary elements.

Plans for SMALL GROUP Literature Circles:
Students participate in SMALL group Literature Circles based upon their novel of choice from a pre-selected group of books or textbook section selected by teacher. Each student has a job that is changed when the 5-day cycle ends. See specific processes & procedures in teacher's folder for organization & discussions prior to beginning small group literature circles.

FIRST & SUBSEQUENT DAYS of Circle: See specific procedures in teacher's folder.

On the 6th (& 11th) day, after SHARING time, students will determine NEW jobs for the next 5-day cycle. NEW JOB SHEETS are distributed before beginning the day's reading so students are aware of the new skill they will be focusing on during reading.

JOBS/SKILLS: (Teacher inserts jobs/skills to be reinforced.)

EXPECTATIONS for ORGANIZATION & BEING ON TASK: Within 2 minutes, groups should be seated at their designated table, with books & folder. Materials needed for jobs should be distributed and group begins "Sharing Time" (discussions of jobs) for approximately 5-8 minutes. Then the group reads together. During the last 8-10 minutes of class, students complete jobs quietly & independently.

TEACHER DAILY ASSESSMENT: Each group has a folder that contains a "Checker's Daily & 5-Day Cycle Report…TEACHER" sheet. Two grades per student are given based on daily participation and cooperation & the quality and completion of his/her job within the 5-day cycle. See "Checker's Daily and 5-Day Cycle Report…Teacher" for details on grading.

ASSESSMENT: A variety of assessment options are available. If the textbook is being used, content area teachers should use the test that coincides with the curriculum.

Sunshine State Standards

LA.A. 1.3.1 Predictions
LA.A. 1.3.2 Conclusions & Inferences
LA.A. 1.3.3 Vocabulary/Words in Context
LA.A 1.3.4 Comprehension
LA.A. 2.3.1 Main Idea & Details
LA.A. 2.3.2 Author's Purpose/Point of View
LA.A. 2.3.5 Locates/Organizes Information
LA.A. 2.3.6 Uses Reference Materials
LA.A 2.3.7 Compare/ Contrast
LA.A. 2.3.8 Fact Opinion, Weak/Strong Arguments
LA.C. 1.3.2 Listens to readings
LA.C. 1.3.4 Summarizing/Paraphrasing
LA.D. 1.3.4 Poetry Techniques
LA.D. 1.3.5 Identifies Common Themes in Literature
LA.E. 1.3.2 Plot/Setting/Conflict Resolution
LA.E. 1.3.3 Figurative Language
LA.E. 2.2.1 Cause & Effect
LA.E. 2.3.1 Character
LA.E. 2.3.3 Responses to text
LA.E. 2.3.7 Reading for personal pleasure

ESOL Strategies

Activate Background Knowledge
Adult/Peer Tutor
Audio/Visual
Cooperative Learning
Direct Instruction
Graphic Organizers
Computer-Technology
Manipulatives
Realia
Self/Peer Assessment
Vocab. Development

ESE MODIFICATIONS

Alternate Evaluation
Extra Time
Flexible Scheduling
Hardcopy of Notes
Key Points
Manipulatives
Modify Assessments
Organizational Skills/Strategies Peer Tutor
Preferential Seating
Proximity Control
Redirection
Test Preview
Use of computer proj.
Use of Planner
Wait Time
Graphic Organizers
Co-operative Groups

MEETINGS:
Mon:

Tues

Wed:

Thur:

Fri:

HOMEWORK:

DISMISSAL DUTY:

Instructional Strategies

Plans for SMALL GROUP Literature Circles: Students participate in SMALL group Literature Circles based upon their book of choice from a pre-selected group of books. Each student has a job that is changed when the 5-day cycle ends. See specific processes & procedures in teacher's folder for organization & discussions prior to beginning small group literature circles.

GOAL: All Students will implement effective reading strategies that ensure comprehension and retention of information read in novels or textbook materials.

STUDENT OBJECTIVES: Students will:
1. Discuss, define, & explore unfamiliar words.
2. Draw conclusions and predict text events using previous knowledge & details in the text.
3. Use evidence in the text to verify predictions.
4. Ask relevant, focused, higher level questions to check for comprehension and clarify any misconceptions.
5. Respond to questions & discussion with relevant & focused comments.
6. Paraphrase & summarize information from the text.
7. Identify & analyze literary elements.

FIRST & SUBSEQUENT DAYS of Circle: See specific procedures in teacher's folder.
On the 6th (& 11th) day, after sharing time, students will determine NEW jobs for the next 5-day cycle. NEW JOB SHEETS are distributed before beginning the day's reading so students are aware of their new responsibilities.
JOBS/SKILLS: (Insert jobs/skills to be reinforced.)

EXPECTATIONS for ORGANIZATION & BEING ON TASK: Within 2 minutes, groups should be seated at their designated table, with books & folder. Materials needed for jobs should be distributed and group begins "Sharing Time" (discussions of jobs) for approximately 5-8 minutes. Then the group reads together. During the last 8-10 minutes of class, students do their jobs quietly and independently.
TEACHER ASSESSMENT: Each group has a folder that contains a "Checker's Daily and 5-Day Report...Teacher Sheet". Two grades per student are given based on daily participation/cooperation & the quality & completion of his/her job. See "Checker's Daily and 5-Day Report...Teacher" for details on grading.
END of BOOK ASSESSMENT: A variety of assessment options are available. If the textbook is being used, content area teachers should use the test that coincides with the curriculum.

ORGANIZATIONAL WORKSHEET
SMALL GROUP LITERATURE CIRCLES

TEACHER: Write a Book Choice in each title box (may need more than one sheet). Then write names of students that selected that book as their FIRST CHOICE. Evaluate # of students in each group. If only 1 student is interested, then look at his/her 2nd then 3rd choice for placement. 4-6 students are recommended for each group. If more than 6 are interested in the same book, have 2 groups read the same book if you have enough copies. 3 in a group is doable. If a student's choices do not coincide with created groups, meet with that student. Have him/her review books that have a group & choose one to join. Avoid showing the members of the group; it could sway his/her decision.

BOOK TITLE:

BOOK TITLE:

BOOK TITLE:

BOOK TITLE:

BOOK TITLE:

BOOK TITLE:

SMALL GROUP PROGRESS SHEET
LITERATURE CIRCLE
This sheet is COMPLETED EACH DAY

Title of Book: _____

DATE we STARTED the BOOK: _____

MEMBERS of the GROUP:

_____   _____

_____   _____

_____   _____

EACH DAY, COMPLETE the READING Information below
to indicate your group's progress while reading this book.

Date		Read From Page		To	
Date		Read From Page		To	
Date		Read From Page		To	
Date		Read From Page		To	
Date		Read From Page		To	
Date		Read From Page		To	
Date		Read From Page		To	
Date		Read From Page		To	
Date		Read From Page		To	
Date		Read From Page		To	
Date		Read From Page		To	
Date		Read From Page		To	
Date		Read From Page		To	
Date		Read From Page		To	
Date		Read From Page		To	

RECORD of 5-DAY CYCLE JOB ASSIGNMENTS
SMALL GROUP LITERATURE CIRCLE

- **Staple this sheet** to the **inside BACK** of your **group's folder.**
- List all members of your group in the FIRST COLUMN.
- Write the **dates** in the **second** column:
    " JOBS & Dates of Job Cycles __ to__".
- Then **fill in each person's JOB for the first 5-Day Cycle.**
- Jobs will be **changed every 5 days.**
- In subsequent cycles, you will **fill in** the third & then fourth column when **dates** & **jobs change.**
- **No member should have the same job twice**

Student's Name:	JOBS & Dates of Job Cycles _____ to _____	JOBS & Dates of Job Cycles _____ to _____	JOBS & Dates of Job Cycles _____ to _____

Record of 5-Day Cycle Job Assignments for SMALL GROUP Folder

Literature Circles: The Reading Buddies © 2009

TEACHER'S ROLE: <u>CHECKER ~ SMALL GROUP</u> Literature Circles

- **TEACHER'S SCORING of job sheets** may be done at **any time during the 5-day cycle** (in or out of class). However, it is best to do as much as possible daily to provide immediate feedback or offer suggestions for improvement. Checking sheets regularly improves the quality of students' work. You may not have time to check every group's work in one class session. You can pick up where you left off the next day or do them outside of class. If a student is having difficulty with the job sheet or understanding the skill, staple a **"<u>SEE ME before completing today's section of your job sheet</u>"** note on the student's paper. You should clarify any misconceptions immediately. A template for these SEE ME notes is located in the Appendix.

- **DURING SMALL group reading time, the TEACHER:**
  - Circulates around the room from group to group.
  - While students are reading aloud, he/she sits with/near each group & "Checks" completion of **previous day's assignments** in folders (which also includes the information shared at the beginning of class).
  - Scores each student's "job" sheet section: maximum 20 points/day.
  - Writes score on the student's Job Sheet.
  - Writes the score for each student under Job Quality & Completion (1 box per day) on **"CHECKER'S DAILY & 5-DAY CYCLE REPORT ...TEACHER".** This is found on the next page.
  - If any student is off task, put a minus - under Participate/Cooperate & encourage student(s) to refocus. You may choose to put a + to positively reinforce being on task or explain that an empty box means a job well done.

- **END of the 5-DAY CYCLE:** Using information from "CHECKER'S DAILY & 5-DAY CYCLE REPORT...TEACHER", the teacher determines 2 grades per week based on:
  - **Daily participation/cooperation points** 100-10 for each minus = participation grade. You can determine your own value for each minus -.
  - **Job quality grade** Add daily points/ day on weekly job sheet to determine grade. 20 points per day = 100 per week, so total points = % grade.
  - To keep the folder organized, staple the groups' completed job sheets together at the end of each 5-Day Cycle.

Enjoy the students interacting with one another
Listen in on their discussions.
Praise them often.
Have high expectations for work habits & behavior.
Students will rise to the occasion!

SMALL GROUP CHECKER'S DAILY & 5-DAY REPORT... <u>TEACHER</u>

As groups are reading, **teacher** circulates around the room **listening,
grading job assignments,** and **evaluating participation**.

This sheet is stapled to the inside front of the group's folder.

Book: _____ **Author**: _____

Dates of 5-Day Cycle: _____

GROUP MEMBERS	YOUR JOB THIS WEEK	PARTICIPATE & COOPERATE					JOB QUALITY & COMPLETION					PARTICIPATE COOPERATE 5-Day Cycle GRADE	JOB 5-Day Cycle GRADE

<u>PARTICIPATE/COOPERATE GRADE:</u> DAILY: + OR a BLANK box designates appropriate participation & behavior (100%)
Minus - is given if a student displays inappropriate behavior. The 5-DAY CYCLE GRADE is REDUCED for EACH minus - . The % amount will be announced by the teacher.

<u>JOB QUALITY GRADE</u>: 20 points are earned for each day's job (completion & quality of work). Total of 100 points can be earned for the 5-Day Cycle.
          Total points = % grade for JOB QUALITY 5-Day Cycle GRADE.

Teacher's Comments: _____

_____

SMALL Group Literature Circles BEGIN TODAY…

Your GROUP needs:
- Your Literature Circle **FOLDER**
- A **copy** of your **BOOK** for **EACH person & 1 EXTRA FOR ME if available.**

☐ **ALL PERSONAL BELONGINGS** should be **ON the FLOOR** **UNDER your table or chair.**

☐ **Put your FOLDER and JOB SHEETS in the MIDDLE of the TABLE.**
 IF APPLICABLE, the ONLY JOB SHEETS OUT DURING READING are:
- **LEXICOGRAPHER**
- **LITERARY ENLIGHTENER**

☐ **BEGIN reading:**
- **Follow along** in your book.
- **Pay attention** to the selection as others read.

☐ **You will do YOUR JOB in the LAST 8-10 minutes of class. I will announce when to begin your job. You will SHARE your job at the beginning of class TOMORROW.**

☐ **CLEAN UP your work area.**

☐ **RETURN FOLDERS & BOOKS** to their **designated places.**

Enjoy your Circle Time!

NOTE to Teacher:
DISPLAY these DIRECTIONS as students enter on the FIRST day of SMALL group circles.

SMALL Group Literature Circles BEGIN Today   Literature Circles: The Reading Buddies © 2009
37

SMALL Group Literature Circles CONTINUE TODAY...
You're doing a FABULOUS JOB!

Your GROUP needs:
- Your Literature Circle **FOLDER**
- A **copy** of your **BOOK** for **EACH person & 1 EXTRA FOR ME if available.**

☐ **ALL PERSONAL BELONGINGS** should be **ON the FLOOR** UNDER your table or chair.

☐ For the **1st 5 - 8 minutes of class....** each person **SHARES his/her work** from the **job sheet. Start** your **discussion promptly.**

☐ **Put** your **FOLDER** and **JOB SHEETS** in the **MIDDLE** of the **TABLE.**
  IF APPLICABLE, the **ONLY JOB SHEETS OUT DURING READING** are:
  - **LEXICOGRAPHER**
  - **LITERARY ENLIGHTENER**

☐ **BEGIN reading:**
  - **Follow along** in your book.
  - **Pay attention** to the selection as others read.

☐ **You will do YOUR JOB** in the **LAST 8 - 10 minutes** of **class. I will announce** when to **begin** your **job. You will SHARE** your **job** at the **beginning** of class **TOMORROW.**

☐ **CLEAN UP your work area.**

☐ **RETURN FOLDERS & BOOKS** to their **designated places.**

Enjoy your Circle Time!

NOTE to Teacher: DISPLAY these DIRECTIONS on SUBSEQUENT days of SMALL group circles.
SMALL Group Literature Circles CONTINUE Today   Literature Circles: The Reading Buddies © 2009

LITERATURE CIRCLE JOBS

To accommodate a 5-Day Cycle,
there are 2 pages for each job sheet.
The 2 pages should be copied back-to-back
so the complete cycle is on one sheet of paper.

~~DIDACTIC DETECTIVE~~
CAUSES (Events) and EFFECTS (Consequences-Results)   Side 1

To be done **AFTER** READING, **NOT** while you are reading.

Student's Name: _____ Book Title: _____

DIDACTIC DETECTIVE: Didactic means "intended to teach or guide". Your job is to teach others about **CAUSE (event) and EFFECT (Consequence-result) Relationships** in the selection EACH day.

Use COMPLETE SENTENCES to explain your causes & effects.

TODAY'S Date: _____ READ from page ___to ___ DATE SHARED: _____

CAUSES (Events)   EFFECTS (Consequences-Results)

#1_____ → #1_____

_____   _____

_____   _____

#2_____ → #2_____

_____   _____

Use COMPLETE SENTENCES to explain your causes & effects.

TODAY'S Date: _____ READ from page ___to ___ DATE SHARED: _____

CAUSES (Events)   EFFECTS (Consequences-Results)

#1_____ → #1_____

_____   _____

_____   _____

#2_____ → #2_____

_____   _____

See BACK SIDE for the NEXT 3 days ⟹

SKILL: Cause and Effect   Literature Circles: The Reading Buddies © 2009

DIDACTIC DETECTIVE'S Name: _____ Side 2

Use COMPLETE SENTENCES to explain your causes & effects.

TODAY'S Date: _____ READ from page ___ to ___ DATE SHARED: _____

CAUSES (Events)   EFFECTS (Consequences-Results)_

#1_____   ⟶   #1_____

_____   _____

#2_____   ⟶   #2_____

_____   _____

Use COMPLETE SENTENCES to explain your causes & effects.

TODAY'S Date: _____ READ from page ___ to ___ DATE SHARED: _____

CAUSES (Events)   EFFECTS (Consequences-Results)_

#1_____   ⟶   #1_____

_____   _____

#2_____   ⟶   #2_____

_____   _____

Use COMPLETE SENTENCES to explain your causes & effects.

TODAY'S Date: _____ READ from page ___ to ___ DATE SHARED: _____

CAUSES (Events)   EFFECTS (Consequences-Results) _

#1_____   ⟶   #1_____

_____   _____

#2_____   ⟶   #2_____

_____   _____

SKILL: Cause and Effect   Literature Circles: The Reading Buddies © 2009

DISCUSSION DELIBERATOR

Side 1

Higher Level Thinking Questions

To be done **AFTER** READING, **NOT** while you are reading.

Student's Name: _____ Book Title: _____

<u>Discussion Deliberator</u>: Your job is to create **two** (2) interesting **HIGHER LEVEL THINKING questions EACH DAY.** Your questions should enhance comprehension &/or stimulate thought provoking discussions. *You may use the <u>Question Cue Card</u> for ideas.*

TODAY'S Date: _____ READ from **page** _____ to _____ DATE SHARED: _____

QUESTION # 1: _____

_____

_____

QUESTION # 2: _____

_____

_____

After SHARING TIME, <u>EXPLAIN</u> what the group discussed & provide specific examples.

_____

_____

TODAY'S Date: _____ READ from **page** _____ to _____ DATE SHARED: _____

QUESTION # 1: _____

_____

_____

QUESTION # 2: _____

_____

_____

After SHARING TIME, <u>EXPLAIN</u> what the group discussed & provide specific examples.

_____

_____

See BACK SIDE for the NEXT 3 days ══════════➤

SKILL: Comprehension with Higher Level Thinking Skills   Literature Circles: The Reading Buddies © 2009

DISCUSSION DELIBERATOR'S Name: _____ Side 2

TODAY'S Date: _____ READ from page _____ to _____ DATE SHARED:_____

QUESTION # 1:_____

_____

_____

QUESTION # 2:_____

_____

_____

After SHARING TIME, EXPLAIN what the group discussed & provide specific examples.

_____

_____

TODAY'S Date: _____ READ from page _____ to _____ DATE SHARED: _____

QUESTION # 1:_____

_____

_____

QUESTION # 2:_____

_____

_____

After SHARING TIME, EXPLAIN what the group discussed & provide specific examples.

_____

_____

TODAY'S Date: _____ READ from page _____ to _____ DATE SHARED:_____

QUESTION # 1:_____

_____

_____

QUESTION # 2:_____

_____

_____

After SHARING TIME, EXPLAIN what the group discussed & provide specific examples.

_____

_____

SKILL: Comprehension with Higher Level Thinking Skills   Literature Circles: The Reading Buddies © 2009

QUESTION CUE CARD
for
DISCUSSION DELIBERATOR

You may use these questions as a GUIDE to create your own
HIGHER LEVEL, THOUGHT PROVOKING QUESTIONS.

As you write your question, add information that relates to your story.

Remember...you can create your OWN higher level, thought provoking questions.
Detail questions are NOT higher level thinking questions.

- What are the implications of _____?
- Why is _____ important?
- What is another way to look at _____?
- What specific conclusions can be drawn from _____?
- How would you explain why _____occurred?
- What might be a metaphor or analogy for _____?
- What might happen if _____?
- How are you like or unlike the main character?
- How are _____ & _____ alike?
- How are _____ & _____ different from each other?
- Explain why you think the author had _____ happen in the story?
- Explain how the story would have changed IF the author had not let__ happen?
- Do you think _____happening will be important later on in the story? **WHY**?
  (This question pertains to the literary element: "foreshadowing"~ something
  said or done that provides a clue to something that might happen later in the
  text.)
- If you would have been _____, how would you have _____?
- What do you think caused _____?
- How do you feel about _____ and why?

~ ELEMENTAL ARTIST ~   Side 1

To be done <u>AFTER</u> READING, <u>NOT while you are reading</u>.

Student's Name: _____ Book Title: _____

<u>Elemental Artist:</u> Your job is to **depict a DIFFERENT story ELEMENT from EACH** day's **reading.** You may **choose** from these story elements:...a <u>**Character**</u> ...the <u>**Setting**</u> ...a <u>**Problem**</u>
...an exciting <u>**Event**</u>/<u>**Surprise**</u> in the story
These elements are depicted at the end of the book: <u>**Climax**</u> (turning point)... <u>**Resolution**</u>

TODAY'S Date: _____ READ from **page** _____ to _____ DATE SHARED: _____

(Circle) the **STORY ELEMENT:**

-CHARACTER	-SETTING	-PROBLEM	-EVENT
	-CLIMAX	-RESOLUTION	

Explain the drawing: _____

WHY is this **important** to the story? _____

_____

TODAY'S Date: _____ READ from **page** _____ to _____ DATE SHARED: _____

(Circle) the **STORY ELEMENT:**

-CHARACTER	-SETTING	-PROBLEM	-EVENT
	-CLIMAX	-RESOLUTION	

Explain the drawing: _____

WHY is this **important** to the story? _____

_____

See BACK SIDE for the NEXT 3 days =========>
SKILLS: Story Elements; Conflict/Resolution; Main Idea; Details; Plot Development

Literature Circles: The Reading Buddies © 2009

ELEMENTAL ARTIST'S Name: _____

TODAY'S Date: _____ READ from **page** ___ to ___ DATE SHARED: _____

(Circle) the STORY ELEMENT:

-CHARACTER	-SETTING	-PROBLEM	-EVENT
	-CLIMAX	-RESOLUTION	

Explain the drawing: _____

WHY is this **important** to the story? _____

_____

TODAY'S Date: _____ READ from **page** _____ to _____ DATE SHARED:

_____

(Circle) the STORY ELEMENT:

-CHARACTER	-SETTING	-PROBLEM	-EVENT
	-CLIMAX	-RESOLUTION	

Explain the drawing: _____

WHY is this **important** to the story? _____

_____

TODAY'S Date: _____ READ from **page** ___ to _____ DATE SHARED: _____

(Circle) the STORY ELEMENT:

-CHARACTER	-SETTING	-PROBLEM	-EVENT
	-CLIMAX	-RESOLUTION	

Explain the drawing: _____

WHY is this **important** to the story?_____

_____

Skills: Story Elements: Conflict/Resolution; Main Idea; Details; Plot Development

Literature Circles: The Reading Buddies © 2009

LEXICOGRAPHER
Side 1

Vocabulary Develop First 2 columns are to be done **DURING** READING,
then the **rest is completed during your job time**.

Student's Name: _____ Book Title: _____

LEXICOGRAPHER: Your job is to create a vocabulary dictionary while reading. Write the **PAGE, PARAGRAPH, & WORD(s)** that you or your group finds challenging, thought provoking, puzzling, or unfamiliar while reading. During job time, you will look them up in a **dictionary & thesaurus** (use computer website, if available) and **complete the chart for EACH day**. If you cannot find a synonym or antonym, your team should help you WITH clues from the definition or context clues. During sharing time, DISCUSS your information rather than merely reading from this sheet.

On the chart **Pg / P = Page / Paragraph #**
Be sure the definition fits the word in the story context.

TODAY'S Date: _____ READ from **page** ___ to ___ DATE SHARED: _____

Pg /P	WORD	DICTIONARY DEFINITION that Fits the CONTEXT	Part of Speech	SYNONYM	ANTONYM

TODAY'S Date: _____ READ from **page** ___ to _____ DATE SHARED: _____

Pg /P	WORD	DICTIONARY DEFINITION that Fits the CONTEXT	Part of Speech	SYNONYM	ANTONYM

See BACK SIDE for the NEXT 3 days ═══════════════════➤

SKILLS: Vocabulary Development; Dictionary/Thesaurus; Context Clues; Synonyms; Antonyms; Parts of Speech
Literature Circles: The Reading Buddies © 2009

Vocabulary Develop First 2 columns are to be done **DURING** READING,
then the **rest is completed during your job time.**

Student's Name: _____ Book Title: _____

TODAY'S Date: _____ **READ** from **page** ___ to ___ **DATE SHARED:** _____

Pg /P	WORD	DICTIONARY DEFINITION that Fits the CONTEXT	Part of Speech	SYNONYM	ANTONYM

TODAY'S Date: _____ **READ** from **page** ___ to ____ **DATE SHARED:** _____

Pg /P	WORD	DICTIONARY DEFINITION that Fits the CONTEXT	Part of Speech	SYNONYM	ANTONYM

TODAY'S Date: _____ **READ** from **page** ___ to ____ **DATE SHARED:** _____

Pg /P	WORD	DICTIONARY DEFINITION that Fits the CONTEXT	Part of Speech	SYNONYM	ANTONYM

See BACK SIDE for the NEXT 3 days ═══════════════════⟹

SKILLS: Vocabulary Development; Dictionary/Thesaurus; Context Clues; Synonyms; Antonyms; Parts of Speech

Literature Circles: The Reading Buddies © 2009

LITERARY ENLIGHTENER   Side 1
Thought Provoking Section of the Text

The **PAGE & PARAGRAPH #** is done <u>**DURING**</u> READING. The **rest** is finished **during job time.**

Student's Name: _____ Book Title: _____

<u>LITERARY ENLIGHTENER</u>: You will locate a thought provoking section of the text.

- ❖ <u>**DURING**</u> reading, **YOU ONLY write** the **page & paragraph #** on this sheet.
- ❖ <u>**AFTER**</u> **reading,** write the lines from the text that you will share with your group. Then **EXPLAIN WHY** you chose the selection.
- ❖ **Suggestions for choosing each section:**
    - ❑ **FIGURATIVE LANGUAGE**: simile, metaphor, onomatopoeia , idiom
    - ❑ **TONE**: author's attitude or opinion through words or actions of characters
    - ❑ **THOUGHT-PROVOKING**: the lines encourage higher-level thinking
    - ❑ **ANALYZING WORDS in TEXT**: giving the text meaning beyond what it tells you directly
    - ❑ **IMAGERY**: text that create a visual imagine

TODAY'S Date: _____ READ from **page** ____ to ____ DATE SHARED:_____
<u>Selection</u>: Page #:____ Paragraph #:____ Suggestion you chose:_____

Words from the text:_____
_____
_____

Explain why you selected this section._____
_____
_____

TODAY'S Date: _____ READ from **page** ____ to ____ DATE SHARED:_____
<u>Selection</u>: Page #:____ Paragraph #:_____ Suggestion you chose_____

Words from the text: _____
_____
_____

Explain why you selected this section. _____
_____
_____

See BACK SIDE for the NEXT 3 days _____➡

SKILL: Figurative Language; Mood; Tone; Analyzing Text; Imagery

Literature Circles: The Reading Buddies © 2009

❖**Suggestions for choosing each selection:**
- ❏ **FIGURATIVE LANGUAGE**: simile, metaphor, onomatopoeia , idiom
- ❏ **MOOD**: humorous, sad, frightening, suspenseful, mysterious
- ❏ **TONE**: author's attitude or opinion through words or actions of characters
- ❏ **THOUGHT-PROVOKING**: the lines encourage higher-level thinking
- ❏ **ANALYZING WORDS in TEXT**: giving the text meaning beyond what it tells you directly
- ❏ **IMAGERY**: text that create a visual imagine

TODAY'S Date: _____ **READ** from **page** ___ to ___ **DATE SHARED:**_____
Selection: Page #:___ Paragraph #:___ Suggestion you chose:_____
Words from the text: _____
_____
_____

Explain why you selected this section._____
_____
_____

TODAY'S Date: _____ **READ** from **page** ___ to ___ **DATE SHARED:**_____
Selection: Page #:___ Paragraph #:___ Suggestion you chose:_____
Words from the text: _____
_____
_____

Explain why you selected this section._____
_____
_____

TODAY'S Date: _____ **READ** from **page** ___ to ___ **DATE SHARED:**_____
Selection: Page #:___ Paragraph #:___ Suggestion you chose:_____
Words from the text: _____
_____
_____

Explain why you selected this section._____
_____
_____

SKILLS: Figurative Language; Mood; Tone; Analyzing Text; Imagery

Literature Circles: The Reading Buddies © 2009

LITERARY LOCKSMITH...Unlocking the Character   Side 1

To be done **AFTER** READING, <u>NOT</u> while you are reading.

Student's Name: _____ Book Title: _____

<u>**LITERARY LOCKSMITH**</u>: Your job is to select a character EACH day & "unlock" information
about the Character so that your group has a key to better understand this character.

<u>Examples of Character **TRAITS**</u> : kind, unkind, ambitious, lazy, brave, courageous,
determined, powerful, obedient, rebellious, leader, follower, strong, weak

<u>Examples of **FEELINGS** (emotions or moods)</u>: love, affection, anger, guilt, depression,
fear, joy, delight, frustration

TODAY'S Date: _____ READ from page ___ to ___ DATE SHARED:_____

Character's Name

The Character's **TRAITS**:
_____
_____
_____

FEELINGS experienced by this
Character: _____
WHY did he/she feel this way?
_____
_____
_____

EXPLAIN how YOU FEEL about this Character.
_____
_____
_____
_____

TODAY'S Date:_____ Read from page ___ to ___ DATE SHARED: _____

Character's Name

The Character's **TRAITS**:
_____
_____
_____

FEELINGS experienced by this
Character: _____
WHY did he/she feel this way?
_____
_____
_____

EXPLAIN how YOU FEEL about this Character.
_____
_____
_____
_____

See BACK SIDE for the NEXT 3 days   ➡

TODAY'S Date: _____   READ from page ____ to ____ DATE SHARED: _____

Character's Name
_____

The Character's **TRAITS**:
_____
_____
_____
_____

FEELINGS experienced by this
Character: _____
WHY did he/she feel this way?

_____
_____

EXPLAIN how YOU FEEL about this Character.
_____
_____
_____

TODAY'S Date:_____   READ from page ____ to ___ DATE SHARED: _____

Character's Name
_____

The Character's **TRAITS**:
_____
_____
_____
_____

FEELINGS experienced by this
Character: _____
WHY did he/she feel this way?

_____
_____

EXPLAIN how YOU FEEL about this Character.
_____
_____
_____

TODAY'S DATE: _____   READ from page ____ to_____   DATE SHARED: _____

Character's Name
_____

The Character's **TRAITS**:
_____
_____
_____

FEELINGS experienced by this
Character: _____
WHY did he/she feel this way?

_____
_____

EXPLAIN how YOU FEEL about this Character.
_____
_____
_____

PLOT PREDICTOR   Side 1
To be done **AFTER** READING, <u>NOT</u> while you are reading.

Student's Name: _____ Book Title: _____

PLOT <u>PREDICTOR</u>: Your job is to predict what you think will happen after reading EACH day. **On Day 2-5** of your job, **you will respond to your predictions from the previous day BEFORE** you make another prediction. You will share during discussion time.

TODAY'S Date: _____ READ from page ___to ___ DATE SHARED:_____

What do you think will happen next? List different possible outcomes.	What is the basis for your predictions? (Why did you make these predictions?)

TODAY'S Date: _____ READ from page ___to ___ DATE SHARED:_____

Use examples from the text to explain how yesterday's predictions were CONFIRMED or UNCONFIRMED.	What do you think will happen next? List different possible outcomes.	What is the basis for your predictions? Why did you make these predictions?)

See BACK SIDE for the NEXT 3 days   ⟶

SKILL: Making Predictions; Drawing Conclusions   Literature Circles The Reading Buddies © 2009

PLOT PREDICTOR'S Name: _____   Side 2

TODAY'S Date: _____ READ from page ___to ___ DATE SHARED:_____

Use examples from the text to explain how yesterday's predictions were CONFIRMED or UNCONFIRMED.	What do you think will happen next? List different possible outcomes.	What is the basis for your predictions? (In other words, why did you make these predictions?)

TODAY'S Date: _____ READ from page___ to ___ DATE SHARED_____

Use examples from the text to explain how yesterday's predictions were CONFIRMED or UNCONFIRMED.	What do you think will happen next? List different possible outcomes.	What is the basis for your predictions? (In other words, why did you make these predictions?)

TODAY'S Date:_____ READ from page ___ to ____ DATE SHARED:_____

Use examples from the text to explain how yesterday's predictions were CONFIRMED or UNCONFIRMED.	What do you think will happen next? List different possible outcomes.	What is the basis for your predictions? (In other words, why did you make these predictions?)	How did the process of making & revisiting predictions help you to understand the story?

STORY CARTOGRAPHER

Side 1

Story Map for 5-Day Cycle

To be done <u>AFTER</u> READING, <u>NOT</u> while you are reading.

Student's Name: _____ Book Title: _____

<u>STORY CARTOGRAPHER</u>: A cartographer creates maps. Your job is to create a STORY MAP about what you've read. There may not be a solution/outcome each day. You will share your story map during your group's discussion time.

TODAY'S Date: _____ **READ** from **page** ___ **to** ___ DATE SHARED: _____

Setting (Where & when):	Important Event 1:	Solution/Outcome
Main Characters:	Important Event 2:	
Plot (Problem-Situation):	Important Event 3:	

TODAY'S Date: _____ **READ** from **page** _____ **to** _____ DATE SHARED: _____

Setting (Where & when):	Important Event 1:	Solution/Outcome
Main Characters:	Important Event 2:	
Plot (Problem-Situation):	Important Event 3:	

See BACK SIDE for the NEXT 3 days ⟶

Skill: Story Elements; Plot Development; Main Idea; Details; Conflict/Resolution

Literature Circles: The Reading Buddies © 2009

STORY CARTOGRAPHER'S Name: _____   Side 2

TODAY'S Date: _____ READ from page ____to ___ DATE SHARED: _____

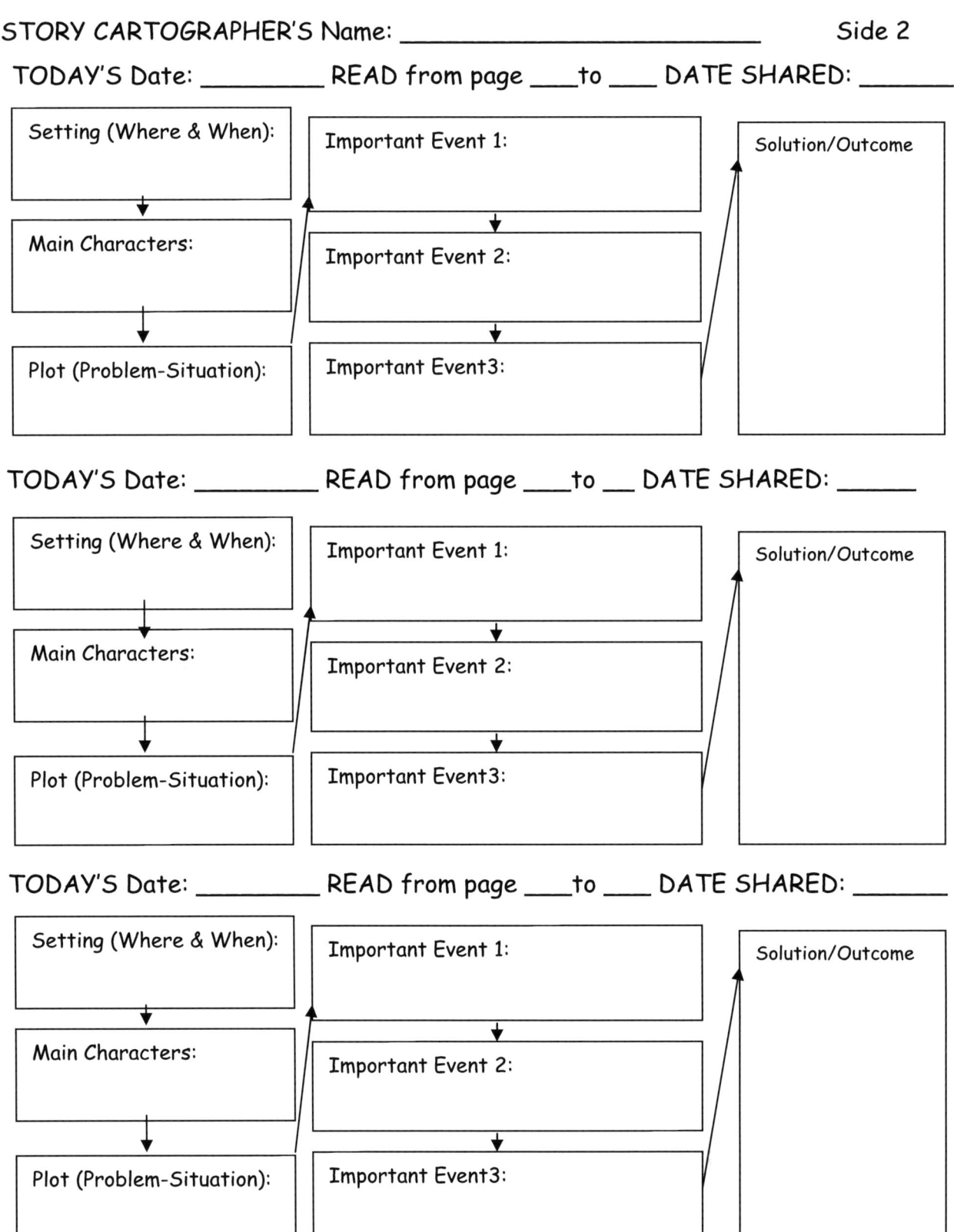

Setting (Where & When):	Important Event 1:	Solution/Outcome
Main Characters:	Important Event 2:	
Plot (Problem-Situation):	Important Event3:	

TODAY'S Date: _____ READ from page ____to __ DATE SHARED: _____

Setting (Where & When):	Important Event 1:	Solution/Outcome
Main Characters:	Important Event 2:	
Plot (Problem-Situation):	Important Event3:	

TODAY'S Date: _____ READ from page ____to ____ DATE SHARED: _____

Setting (Where & When):	Important Event 1:	Solution/Outcome
Main Characters:	Important Event 2:	
Plot (Problem-Situation):	Important Event3:	

Skill: Story Elements; Plot Development; Main Idea; Details; Conflict/Resolution

Literature Circles: The Reading Buddies © 2009

STORY RECAPITULATOR

Side 1

Brief Summary

Student's Name: _____ Book Title:_____

To be done **AFTER** READING, **NOT** while you are reading.

RECAPITULATOR: You will write a **brief SUMMARY (recap)** of what the group reads **EACH day**. It should focus on the highlights or **important ideas** of what you read, including the **key events**. You will share your summary during your group's discussion time.

TODAY'S Date: _____ READ from **page** _____ to _____ DATE SHARED: _____

Write your **summary (recap)** of today's reading: _____

_____

_____

_____

_____

_____

_____

_____

_____

_____

TODAY'S Date: _____ READ from **page** _____ to _____ DATE SHARED: _____

Write your **summary (recap)** of today's reading: _____

_____

_____

_____

_____

_____

_____

_____

_____

_____

See BACK SIDE for the NEXT 3 days ➡

SKILL: Comprehension: Main Idea; Details; Summarizing Key Events

Literature Circles: The Reading Buddies © 2009

STORY RECAPITULATOR'S Name: _____ Side 2

TODAY'S Date: _____ READ from **page** ___ to ___ DATE SHARED: _____

Write your **summary (recap)** of today's reading: _____

_____

_____

_____

_____

_____

_____

_____

_____

TODAY'S Date: _____ READ from **page** _____to_____ DATE SHARED: _____

Write your **summary (recap)** of today's reading: _____

_____

_____

_____

_____

_____

_____

_____

_____

_____

TODAY'S Date: _____ READ from **page** _____to_____ DATE SHARED: _____

Write your **summary (recap)** of today's reading: _____

_____

_____

_____

_____

_____

_____

_____

_____

SKILL: Comprehension: Main Idea; Details; Summarizing Key Events

TEXT CONNECTOR   Side 1

To be done **AFTER** READING, **NOT** while you are reading.

Student's Name: _____ Book Title:_____

TEXT CONNECTOR: Your job is to make **one** interesting **connection**, **EACH DAY**, between your reading (text) & the world beyond the book. You will explain how the characters, setting, or events in the **TEXT** relate (connect) to one of these choices:
- ❑ to **SELF** (your life, your friends),
- ❑ to **WORLD** (other people, problems, events),
- ❑ to **TEXT** (another book or story that you've read).

Be **specific** & **thorough** so that we understand the **reason** for your connection.

CIRCLE the type of connection you make each day, & use complete sentences.

TODAY'S Date: _____ READ from page ___to_____ DATE SHARED: _____

CONNECTION: (CIRCLE) the connection you made: TEXT to | SELF... WORLD...TEXT |

_____

_____

_____

_____

_____

_____

TODAY'S Date: _____ READ from page _____to _____ DATE SHARED: _____

CONNECTION: (CIRCLE) the connection you made: TEXT to | SELF...WORLD... TEXT |

_____

_____

_____

_____

_____

_____

See BACK SIDE for the NEXT 3 days =======➤

SKILL: Making Personal Connections to Text   Literature Circles: The Reading Buddies © 2009

TEXT CONNECTOR'S Name:_____   Side 2

TODAY'S Date: _____ READ from page _____to_____ DATE SHARED: _____

CONNECTION: CIRCLE the connection you made: TEXT to | SELF...WORLD...TEXT |

_____
_____
_____
_____
_____
_____
_____

TODAY'S Date: _____ READ from page _____to_____ DATE SHARED: _____

CONNECTION: CIRCLE the connection you made: TEXT to | SELF...WORLD...TEXT |

_____
_____
_____
_____
_____
_____
_____

TODAY'S Date: _____ READ from page _____to_____ DATE SHARED: _____

CONNECTION: CIRCLE the connection you made: TEXT to | SELF...WORLD...TEXT |

_____
_____
_____
_____
_____
_____
_____

SKILL: Making Personal Connections to Text   Literature Circles: The Reading Buddies © 2009

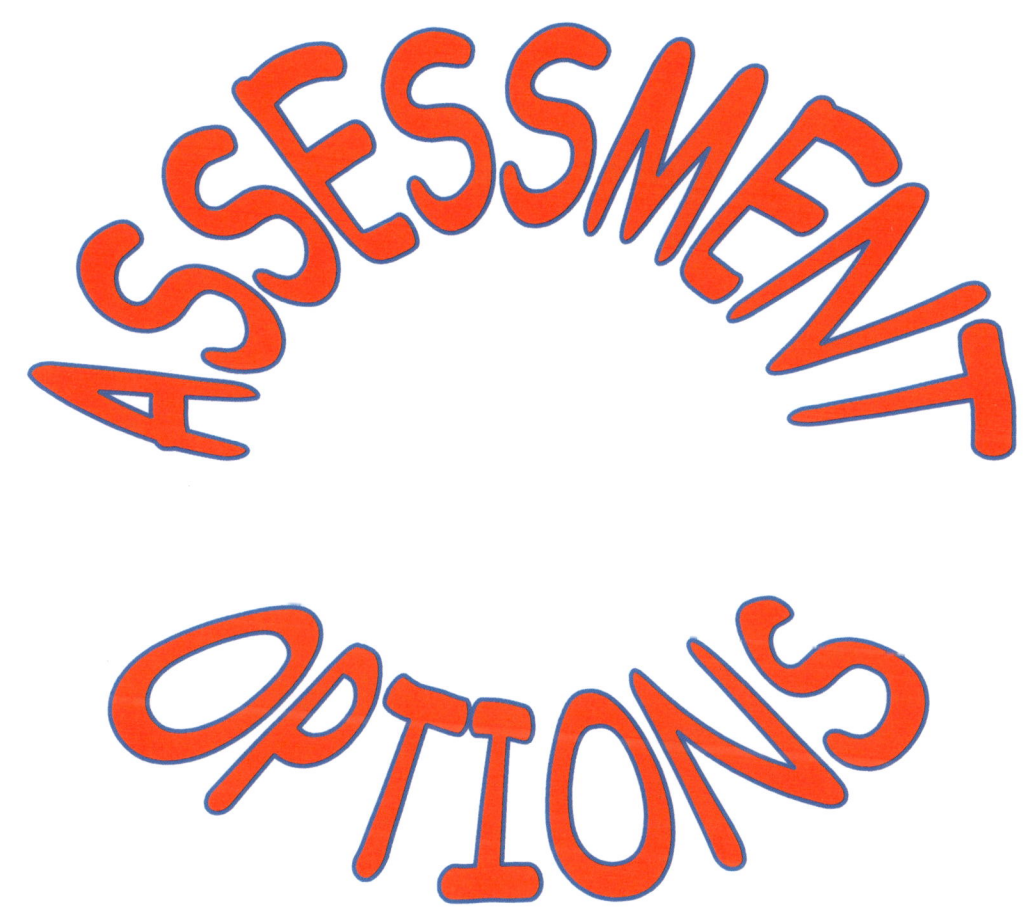

ASSESSMENT OPTIONS

GREAT IDEAS for End of Book Activities or Tests
ASSESSMENT OPTIONS

1. If you have the **Accelerated Reader Tests Computer Program (AR Tests)**:

   ❑ Each student takes an AR test.
   ❑ The goal is to read, understand, & enjoy a book. You may consider letting them use their job sheets to discuss the test questions together collaborating to eliminate wrong answers. This is your decision. Be nearby to assure that they are discussing the answers rather than 1 student just supplying the answer to another. This is especially effective for low-level or marginal readers.

2. Create a **Teacher Made Test** or find a test online for the book. We found the easiest method is to search by book title TEST.
   Example: Red Badge of Courage Test

3. If a textbook is being used, content area teachers should use the tests that correlate with their materials.

4. If you choose, groups can work together or independently to complete the **Assessment - End of Book STORY CARTOGRAPHER** for the entire novel, especially if you chose not to use this as a 5-day cycle job. After a WHOLE group circle, the class can do the STORY CARTOGRAPHER ASSESSMENT with the teacher. This provides an opportunity for you to teach/model plot analysis & story elements.

5. Use **ASSESSMENT END of BOOK- CHARACTER COMPARISONS** to compare & contrast the protagonist & antagonist in the novel.

6. Have students write a **BOOK TALK,** which includes a summary of the book, suggested audience, & explanation of why they liked or disliked the book. Then they share the book talk with the class, other classes, or on your school's TV News Broadcast. The group could do this independently or as a cooperative effort. If small literature groups have read different books, Book Talks are a wonderful way to entice other classmates' interest in the book.

7. Students create a **GAME BOARD** or **GAME FORMAT** such as Jeopardy or Tic-Tac-Toe. There are many ideas and rubrics available online. Type in "Book Projects for middle or high school".

CHARACTER COMPARISONS ~~ END OF BOOK ASSESSMENT

Name: _____ Date:_____ Period:____

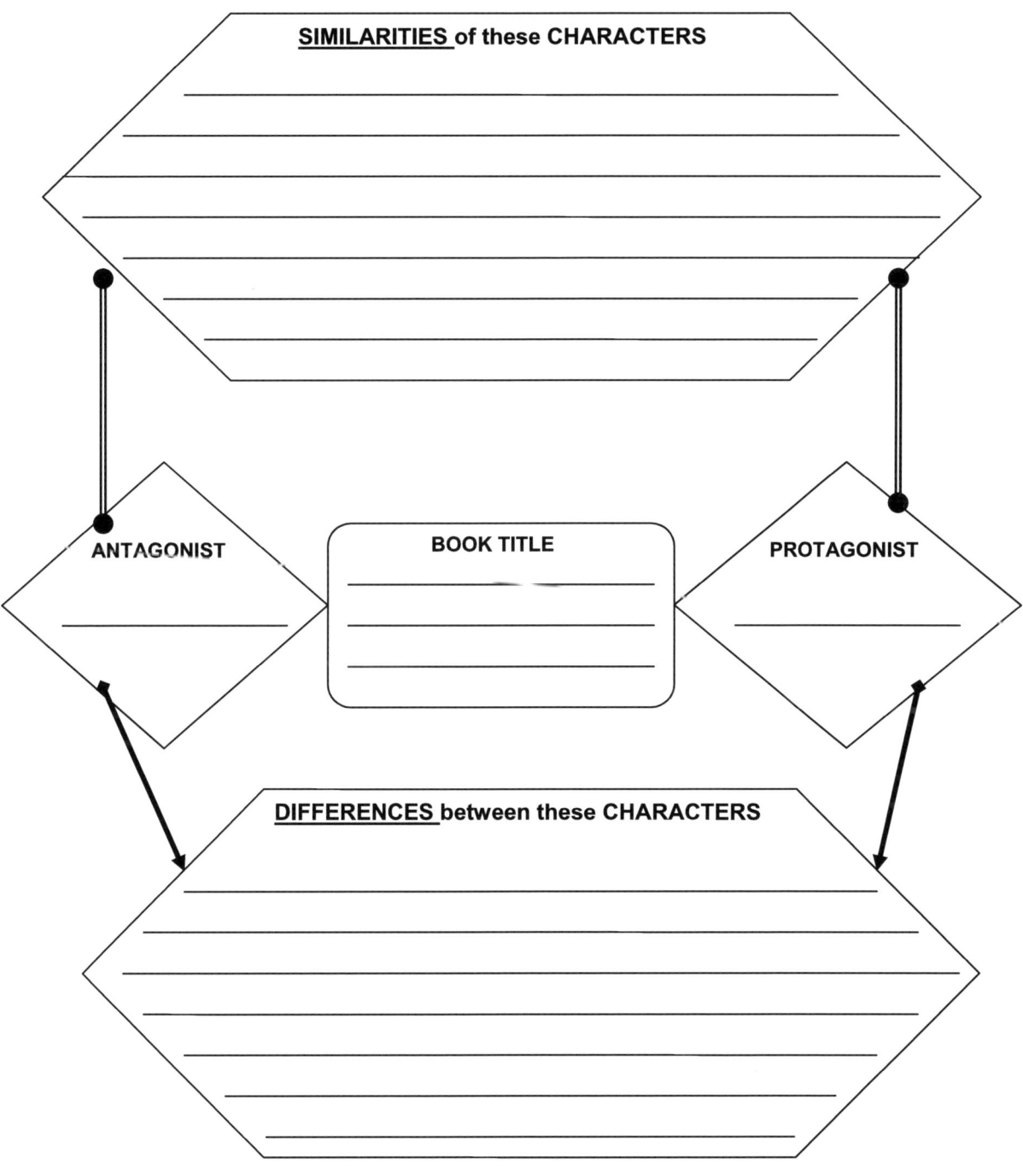

SIMILARITIES of these CHARACTERS

_____

_____

_____

_____

_____

_____

ANTAGONIST

_____

BOOK TITLE

_____

_____

_____

PROTAGONIST

_____

DIFFERENCES between these CHARACTERS

_____

_____

_____

_____

_____

_____

STORY CARTOGRAPHER
END of BOOK ASSESSMENT

Student's Name: _____ Date: _____ Period:____

BOOK TITLE: _____ Author:_____

To be done WHEN the BOOK IS COMPLETED.

<u>START HERE</u> Complete this STORY MAP to demonstrate your understanding
of **story Elements** & **Plot Analysis.**

MAIN CHARACTERS:_____

_____

SETTING (Where & When):

_____

_____

5.

Important Event 5:

_____

_____

6.

CLIMAX (Turning Point):

_____

_____

_____

_____

4.

Important Event 4:

_____

_____

_____

3.

Important Event 3:

_____

_____

_____

7.

**RESOLUTION (How problem
was solved):** _____

_____

_____

_____

2.

Important Event 2:

_____

_____

_____

CONFLICT
(Rising Action)

1.

INITIATING EVENT 1
(Problem-Situation):

_____

_____

_____

8.

DENOUEMENT~CONCLUSION
(Ending): _____

_____

_____

_____

_____

PLOT
DEVELOPMENT

Assessment Skill: Story Elements; Plot Development; Main Idea; Details; Plot Analysis

LITERATURE CIRCLES

APPENDIX

is the recommended age or grade level for your Literature Circle program?
scovered that most available literature circle information was geared toward
...u...ury school. Therefore we designed a format that would appeal to older
students. Our worksheets are designed for use with middle or high school reading,
language arts, and content area classrooms. In addition to the textbook, there are
many historical fiction or non-fiction books available to supplement content area
curriculums.

Q: Is it difficult to begin using Literature Circles?
A: No, we have created a Ready…Set…Teach Program that has all the materials
needed except the books. It's all at your fingertips & ready to use. The materials we
created have been tested in our classrooms, revised, & revised again to provide the
best learning opportunity for students and easy use for teachers.

Q: How long does it take to complete a book in a Literature Circle?
A: Of course, this depends on the length of the book & the amount of time a group
might spend discussing or clarifying information while reading. Most books can be
completed within 2-3 weeks of class time. Textbook chapters or units will vary.

Q: Why do students have JOBS to do rather than just read?
A: The JOBS we have created are based on essential reading skills that incorporate
the   National Council for the Teachers of English (NCTE) Standards. These skills align
with many state's standards as well. We've designed 10 jobs that reinforce 21
essential reading skills to ensure students become more proficient readers. These job
choices help the teacher to identify strengths or weaknesses of individual students and
make necessary instructional changes.

Q: How often should students change jobs?
A: We recommend students continue with the same job for 5 days. This allows them to
become comfortable with the procedures & format as well as using teacher feedback
to improve their responses, enhance understanding of the skills involved, and achieve
mastery.

Q: Should I use all 10 JOBS each week?
A: This is not recommended. It is better to focus on 4-5 jobs at a time. We have
provided a Cross Reference of Reading Skills & Jobs so that you can easily identify
the skills practiced for each job. You should select JOBS that reinforce the skills that
you have taught so that the Literature Circle will provide relevant opportunities to use,
practice, & master these skills.

Q: If a job is not done correctly or isn't quality work, when should I address this
concern with the student?
A: This concern needs to be addressed early in the 5-day cycle. It is best to not
interrupt the students while reading or during sharing time. We recommend attaching a
note to the student's job sheet asking the student to see you prior to completing the
next section of the job sheet. (See Appendix for a See Me template note.)

Q: Why do you have 5 days of a job on 1 sheet of paper?
A: The main reason we organized jobs like this was to save paper, money, & time running so many sheets. Originally we had 1 sheet per day, using both sides of the page. This not only wasted paper, but created too many pieces of paper for each student & teacher to keep track of. After trial and error & tweaking our revisions we organized the job sheets to what we thought would be economical & efficient. It is easy to grade 1 sheet (front & back) for the entire week. Having only 1 sheet per student helps to keep the group's folder organized. On the 5th day, **after sharing**, the teacher or students can staple the week's worth of jobs together so they are not confused with new sheets that are put in the folder. Students have adapted well to the amount of space on each job sheet.

Q: How do I decide on book options for the students?
A: First of all, you need to determine what books are available in your school—ones with multiple copies or class sets. Then take into account the reading level of your students as well as their interest level. There are many websites that offer a list of suggested books by grade level or age range. We've acquired books by writing grants to purchase class sets of books. Our PTO has purchased class sets for us as well. Check to see if your school district has class sets available for check out. Of course if you are using the textbook the selection is already made for you.

Q: How do I decide on which books my students will read?
A: Students with choices (even if they are limited) tend to be more open-minded about reading the book. To empower students to select the literature circle book it is important to provide information to help in their decisions. Creating your own "book talks" about the book selections will provide information to help students determine if they are interested in the book. Be creative & interesting! We suggest you find book reviews that are available online. We have taken the book talk a step further by using a power point presentation with a picture of the book and a review. This allowed us to print a handout of the presentation for students that were absent or for students that wanted to see the book review again. While we are presenting the book & review, students write down the titles & authors of those they are interested in. (See "Books I'd Like to Read" template in the Appendix. Specific suggestions are addressed in the process & procedures sections for both whole and small group circles.

Q: Do I need to have read all the books I use for Literature Circles?
A: Having read the book(s) is advantageous; however, it is not necessary for small or whole group circles. **For SMALL Literature Circles titles:** If you are not familiar with the books, we suggest reading book reviews. **For WHOLE Group Literature Circles:** You will be reading the book with the students. However, reading a chapter ahead is advised. Don't avoid using a wonderful book just because you haven't had the opportunity to read it.

Q: Is there a problem if "friends" are interested in the same book for small group circles?

A: You organize the small groups & know your students well enough to make the correct decisions on group placement. You might be pleasantly surprised. They may work hard to stay together. However, it is important that you are consistent with your expectations & students being on task.

Q: Why is it necessary for my students to be involved with the decisions/expectations for our Literature Circles?

A: Student involvement empowers them to take ownership of the decisions. They are more likely to comply with the expectations. This is explained further in our "Success of the Circle Guidelines" on page 11.

Q: Lit Circles sound great! Is it alright for me to complete other work while the class or groups are reading?

A: Absolutely NOT! If you want to create a positive learning atmosphere producing quality work then you need to be involved. In a whole group, you should be reading along with the students—even modeling great oral reading periodically. It is also a time to model "facilitating" a circle so that students can see how a discussion is conducted during reading as well as clarifying information. During small group Literature Circles, we were moving about the room, grading students' jobs from the previous day, providing feedback with comments or questions on their job sheets, monitoring behavior, being sure groups were on task, and listening to groups read & discuss. We have outlined the teacher's role as CHECKER & provided the necessary monitoring & grading worksheets for you.

Q: I teach social studies. Why should I use your literature program?

 A: Often times content area teachers assume or expect that all students can read & comprehend on grade level text. The facts are that a large portion of your students can fluently read the text, but they are not comprehending nor retaining what they read. Often times we are puzzled when the students do poorly on their exams or fail to complete workbook pages or homework. Our program requires that all students maintain active involvement throughout the reading thus greatly reducing time off task. Using the jobs (reading strategies) plus active collaboration & discussion among students and teacher will greatly increase the students understanding of the text.

Q. How do I give a book talk & get enthusiastic about a textbook?

A. This is an excellent question! Many of our students are lacking in background knowledge of the subject being taught. Prior to starting a section of the text, spend a portion of class or an entire class period providing the students with the much needed background knowledge that will lead them into the reading. Use maps, charts, and artifacts, tell interesting stories, and use personal experiences. Be upbeat & enthusiastic as you are presenting the information.

Q: How can I ask a question, share a comment, or express a concern about Literature Circles?

A: We welcome your questions, concerns, and feedback. You can email your questions or comments to us at: readingbuddies09@yahoo.com We'd love to hear from you and your students!

ABSENT? BOOK CHECK OUT for MAKE-UP WORK

NAME	PERIOD #	TITLE of BOOK	DATE OUT	Date IN

Books I'd Like to Read in the Future

Name: _____ Date: _____

Title: _____ Author: _____

Title: _____ Author: _____

Title: _____ Author: _____

Title: _____ Author: _____

Title: _____ Author: _____

Title: _____ Author: _____

Title: _____ Author: _____

Title: _____ Author: _____

Title: _____ Author: _____

Title: _____ Author: _____

Title: _____ Author: _____

Title: _____ Author: _____

Title: _____ Author: _____

SEE ME before completing today's section of your job sheet.

SEE ME before completing today's section of your job sheet.

SEE ME before completing today's section of your job sheet.

SEE ME before completing today's section of your job sheet.

SEE ME before completing today's section of your job sheet.

SEE ME before completing today's section of your job sheet.

SEE ME before completing today's section of your job sheet.

SEE ME before completing today's section of your job sheet.

SEE ME before completing today's section of your job sheet.

SEE ME before completing today's section of your job sheet.

SEE ME before completing today's section of your job sheet.

SEE ME before completing today's section of your job sheet.

These photos provide examples of organizing
materials & folders, using worksheets,
& completed job sheets.

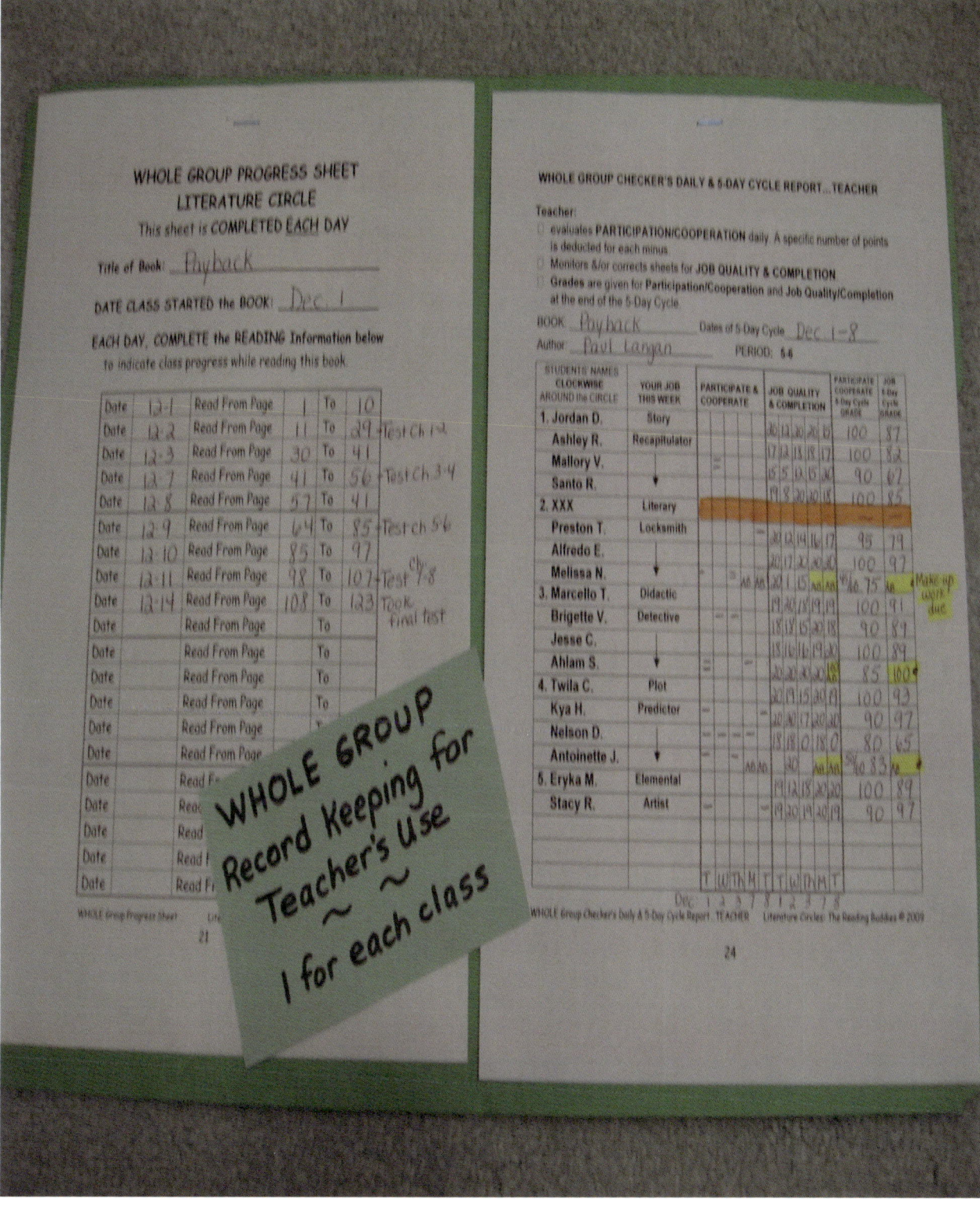

WHOLE GROUP CHECKER'S DAILY & 5-DAY CYCLE REPORT...TEACHER

Teacher:

☐ evaluates **PARTICIPATION/COOPERATION** daily. A specific number of points is deducted for each minus.

☐ Monitors &/or corrects sheets for **JOB QUALITY & COMPLETION**.

☐ **Grades** are given for **Participation/Cooperation** and **Job Quality/Completion** at the end of the 5-Day Cycle.

BOOK: _Payback_   Dates of 5-Day Cycle _Dec. 1–8_

Author: _Paul Langan_   PERIOD: **5-6**

STUDENTS' NAMES CLOCKWISE AROUND the CIRCLE	YOUR JOB THIS WEEK	PARTICIPATE & COOPERATE					JOB QUALITY & COMPLETION					PARTICIPATE COOPERATE 5-Day Cycle GRADE	JOB 5-Day Cycle GRADE
1. Jordan D.	Story						20	12	20	20	15	100	87
Ashley R.	Recapitulator						17	12	18	18	17	100	82
Mallory V.	↓	=					15	5	12	15	20	90	67
Santo R.	▼						19	8	20	20	18	100	85
2. XXX	Literary											~	~
Preston T.	Locksmith					−	20	12	14	16	17	95	79
Alfredo E.							20	17	20	20	20	100	97
Melissa N.	▼	−		=	AB	AB	20	1	15	AB	AB	45/60 75 AB	
3. Marcello T.	Didactic						19	20	18	19	19	100	91
Brigette V.	Detective	−	−				18	18	15	20	18	90	89
Jesse C.	↓						18	16	16	19	20	100	89
Ahlam S.	▼	=			−		20	20	20	20	100 AB	85	100
4. Twila C.	Plot						20	19	15	20	19	100	93
Kya H.	Predictor	−				−	20	20	17	20	20	90	97
Nelson D.	↓	−	−	−	−		18	18	0	18	0	80	65
Antoinette J.	▼	−		−	AB	AB		20		AB	AB	50/60 83 AB	
5. Eryka M.	Elemental						19	12	18	20	20	100	89
Stacy R.	Artist	−				−	19	20	19	20	19	90	97
0 = make up work due		T	W	Th	M	T	T	W	Th	M	T		

Dec: 1   2   3   7   8   1   2   3   7   8

Success of the Circle

1. • Participate actively
2. • Pay attention
3. • Work quietly
4. • Follow along while reading
5. • Share information
6. • Be on task
7. • Be respectful and kind
8. • Listen
9. • Voice your opinion
10. • Disagree politely
11. • Take turns
12. • Begin work promptly

Small Group
Team
Folder

GREAT
IDEAS!

SMALL GROUP PROGRESS SHEET
LITERATURE CIRCLE
This sheet is COMPLETED _EACH_ DAY

Title of Book: _Harriet Tubman- Freedom Leader_
DATE we STARTED the BOOK: _March 2_
MEMBERS of the GROUP:

James C.	Natalie P.
Sara L.	Jason T.

EACH DAY, COMPLETE the READING Information below
to indicate your group's progress while reading this book.

Date	3-2	Read From Page	1	To	11
Date	3-3	Read From Page	12	To	25
Date	3-4	Read From Page	26	To	39
Date	3-5	Read From Page	40	To	53
Date	3-6	Read From Page	54	To	67
Date	3-9	Read From Page	68	To	80
Date	3-10	Read From Page	81	To	92
Date	3-11	Read From Page	93	To	105
Date	3-12	Read From Page	106	To	119
Date	3-13	Read From Page	119	To	133
Date		Read From Page		To	
Date		Read From Page		To	
Date		Read From Page		To	
Date		Read From Page		To	
Date		Read From Page		To	

SMALL GROUP PROGRESS Sheet for Folder   Literature Circles: The Reading Buddies ©2009

33

SMALL GROUP CHECKER'S DAILY & 5-DAY REPORT... _TEACHER_

As groups are reading, teacher circulates around the room listening,
grading job assignments, and evaluating participation.

This sheet is stapled to the inside front of the group's folder.

Book: _Harriet Tubman-Freedom_   Author: _Tanya Savory_
Leader
Dates of 5-Day Cycle: _March 9-13_

GROUP MEMBERS	YOUR JOB THIS WEEK	PARTICIPATE & COOPERATE					JOB QUALITY & COMPLETION					PARTICIPATE COOPERATE 5-Day Cycle GRADE	JOB 5-Day Cycle GRADE
James C.	Plot Predictor	+	-	+	+	+	15	20	18	20	10	90%	83%
Sara L.	Didactic Detective	+	+	+	+	+	20	20	20	20	20	100%	100%
Natalie P.	Story Recapitulator	+	+		-	A +	20	15	10	A 20		-5/80 94%	*
Jason T.	Discussion Deliberator	+	+	+	+	+	20	30	15	20	20	100%	95%

PARTICIPATE/COOPERATE GRADE: DAILY: + OR a BLANK box designates appropriate participation & behavior (100%)
Minus - is given if a student displays inappropriate behavior. The 5-DAY CYCLE GRADE is REDUCED for EACH minus - . The % amount will be announced by the teacher.

JOB QUALITY GRADE: 20 points are earned for each day's job (completion & quality of work).
Total of 100 points can be earned for the 5-Day Cycle.
    Total points = % grade for JOB QUALITY 5-Day Cycle GRADE.

Teacher's Comments: _Fabulous discussion on why Harriet_
wouldn't allow the fugitive to return when the
escape became very difficult. Love the teamwork!

SMALL Group Checker's Daily & 5-Day Report.. Teacher's Evaluation   Literature Circles: The Reading Buddies © 2009
* _Natalie - be sure to turn in_
your work from your absence.
36

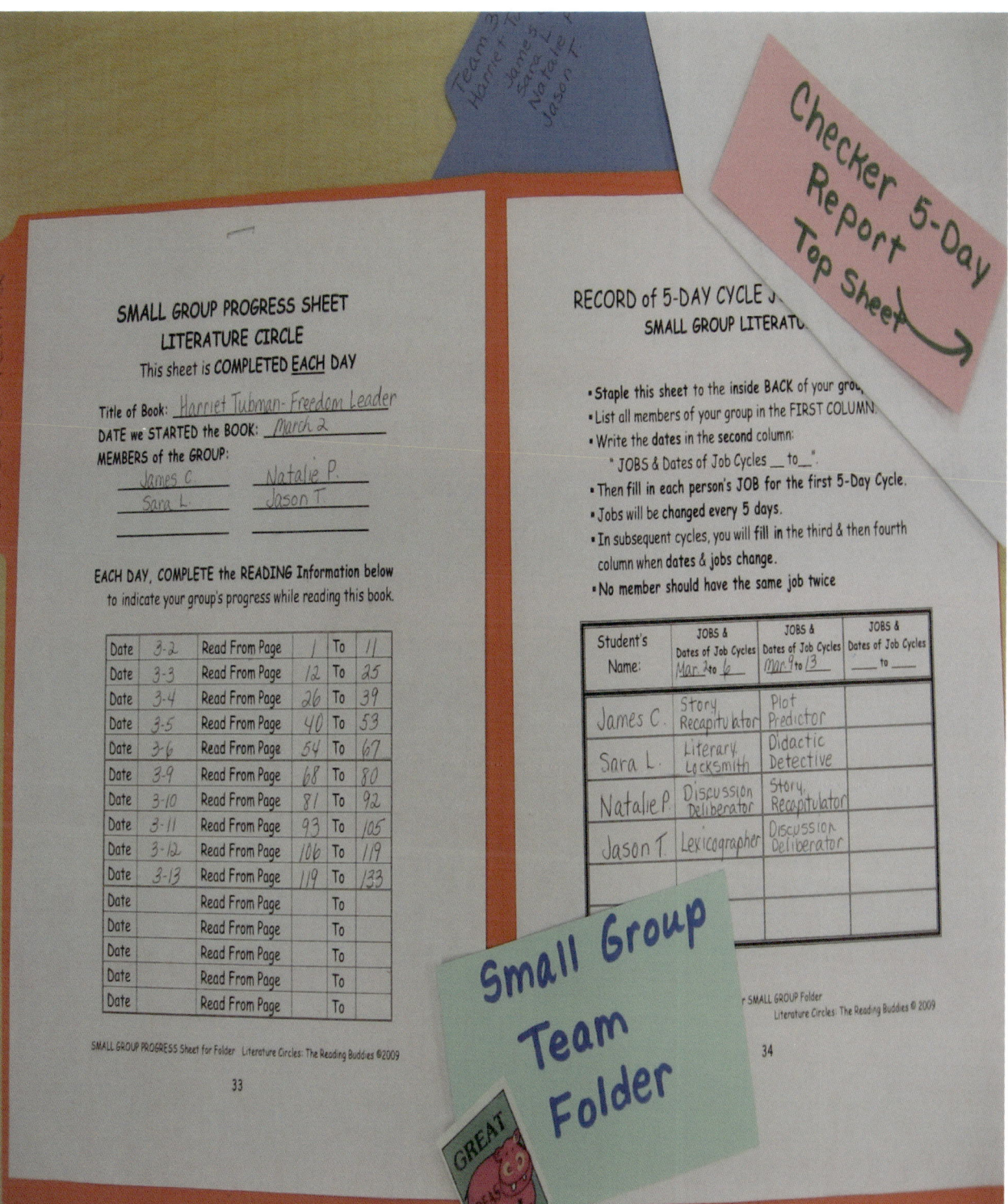

SMALL GROUP PROGRESS SHEET
LITERATURE CIRCLE
This sheet is COMPLETED UNDER DAY

Title of Book: _Harriet Tubman - Freedom Leader_
DATE we STARTED the BOOK: _March 2_
MEMBERS of the GROUP:

James C.   _Natalie P._
Sara L.   _Jason T._
_____   _____

EACH DAY, COMPLETE the READING Information below
to indicate your group's progress while reading this book.

Date	3-2	Read From Page	1	To	11
Date	3-3	Read From Page	12	To	25
Date	3-4	Read From Page	26	To	39
Date	3-5	Read From Page	40	To	53
Date	3-6	Read From Page	54	To	67
Date	3-9	Read From Page	68	To	80
Date	3-10	Read From Page	81	To	92
Date	3-11	Read From Page	93	To	105
Date	3-12	Read From Page	106	To	119
Date	3-13	Read From Page	119	To	133
Date		Read From Page		To	
Date		Read From Page		To	
Date		Read From Page		To	
Date		Read From Page		To	
Date		Read From Page		To	

SMALL GROUP PROGRESS Sheet for Folder   Literature Circles: The Reading Buddies ©2009

33

RECORD of 5-DAY CYCLE J...
SMALL GROUP LITERAT...

• Staple this sheet to the inside BACK of your gro...
• List all members of your group in the FIRST COLUMN.
• Write the dates in the second column:
   " JOBS & Dates of Job Cycles __ to__".
• Then fill in each person's JOB for the first 5-Day Cycle.
• Jobs will be changed every 5 days.
• In subsequent cycles, you will fill in the third & then fourth
   column when dates & jobs change.
• No member should have the same job twice

Student's Name:	JOBS & Dates of Job Cycles _Mar 2 to 6_	JOBS & Dates of Job Cycles _Mar 9 to 13_	JOBS & Dates of Job Cycles ___ to ___
James C.	Story Recapitulator	Plot Predictor	
Sara L.	Literary Locksmith	Didactic Detective	
Natalie P.	Discussion Deliberator	Story Recapitulator	
Jason T.	Lexicographer	Discussion Deliberator	

...r SMALL GROUP Folder
Literature Circles: The Reading Buddies © 2009

34

Checker 5-Day Report Top Sheet →

Small Group Team Folder

GREAT IDEAS

~~DIDACTIC DETECTIVE~~
CAUSES (Events) and EFFECTS (Consequences-Results)   Side 1

To be done **AFTER** READING, **NOT** while you are reading.

Student's Name: _Taylor G._   Book Title: _Payback_

DIDACTIC DETECTIVE: Didactic means "intended to teach or guide". Your job is to teach others about **CAUSE (event) and EFFECT (Consequence-result) Relationships** in the selection EACH day.   _98%_

Use COMPLETE SENTENCES to explain your causes & effects.

TODAY'S Date: _12/1_ READ from page _1_ to _10_ DATE SHARED: _12/2_

CAUSES (Events)	EFFECTS (Consequences-Results)
#1 _When Darrel fought with Tyray._	→ #1 _Tyray got a broken arm._
#2 _Tyray got 3 days suspension._	→ #2 _Tyray got in trouble with his dad._

_+20_
Terrific

Use COMPLETE SENTENCES to explain your causes & effects.

TODAY'S Date: _12/2_ READ from page _11_ to _27_ DATE SHARED: _12/5_

CAUSES (Events)	EFFECTS (Consequences-Results)
#1 _Tyray meets Lark, who is the only one nice to him._	→ #1 _Tyray becomes friends with Lark._ _+20_
#2 _Tyray returns to school_ _Great observation!_	→ #2 _No one is afraid of him anymore._

See BACK SIDE for the NEXT 3 days ➡

SKILL: Cause and Effect   Literature Circles: The Reading Buddies © 2009

81

DISCUSSION DELIBERATOR
Side 1
Higher Level Thinking Questions
To be done **AFTER** READING, **NOT** while you are reading.

Student's Name: _Cheyenne_   Book Title: _Harriet Tubman: Freedom Leader_

Discussion Deliberator: Your job is to create **two** (2) interesting **HIGHER LEVEL THINKING** questions EACH DAY. Your questions should enhance comprehension &/or stimulate thought provoking discussions. *You may use the Question Cue Card for ideas.*

TODAY'S Date: _4/28_   READ from page _1_ to _11_ DATE SHARED: _____ ⊝ -1

QUESTION # 1: If you would have been caught by Miss Sarah with the sugar cube how would you have reacted to the situation? (+19)

QUESTION # 2: How do you feel about the owners beating Harriet with a whip and why?

After SHARING TIME, **EXPLAIN** what the group discussed & provide specific examples.

1. Would've taken the beating, given it back.
2. It's unjust? Everybody's the same? Feel awful   *Good discussion*

TODAY'S Date: _4-29_ ⊝-1 READ from page _12_ to _23_ ⊝-1 DATE SHARED: ⊝-1

QUESTION # 1: What might happen if Harriet does runaway?   +6   (+14)

QUESTION # 2: What do you think caused Harriet to not listen to her father? +6

After SHARING TIME, **EXPLAIN** what the group discussed & provide specific examples.

+3 1. Slave master might **catch** her ? they wouldn't really care ? 50/50 chance *No response for question #2.* (-3)

See BACK SIDE for the NEXT 3 days ➡

~ ELEMENTAL ARTIST ~   Side 1

To be done AFTER READING, NOT while you are reading.

Student's Name: Stacy R.   Book Title: Pay Back

Elemental Artist: Your job is to **depict a DIFFERENT** story **ELEMENT** from **EACH** day's reading. You may **choose** from these story elements:...a **Character** ...the **Setting** ...a **Problem**

...an exciting **Event/Surprise** in the story

These elements are depicted at the end of the book: **Climax** (turning point)... **Resolution**

TODAY'S Date: 12-1   READ from page 1 to 11   DATE SHARED: 12-2

Circle the STORY ELEMENT: (CHARACTER)   -SETTING   -PROBLEM -EVENT
-CLIMAX   -RESOLUTION

Dad   *tyray*

Excellent element to depict!
+20

Explain the drawing: Tyray's dad smaking him because he got suspended

WHY is this important to the story? It shows why tray is all ways so angry all the time and bullying people.

TODAY'S Date: 12-2   READ from page 11 to 29   DATE SHARED: 12-3

Circle the STORY ELEMENT: -CHARACTER   -SETTING   -PROBLEM   (-EVENT) -1
-CLIMAX   -RESOLUTION

tyray meets up
with bones and
discovers that
bones has a gun.

tyray   *bones*

$\frac{+19}{20}$

this was a very important event well done.

Glad you added this!

Explain the drawing: Tyray was thinking about taking the gun to get revenge

WHY is this important to the story? It shows what tyray was thinking about taking the gun to get revenge on dre!!

See BACK SIDE for the NEXT 3 days =========▶

SKILLS: Story Elements; Conflict/Resolution; Main Idea; Details; Plot Development

Literature Circles: The Reading Buddies © 2009

83

LEXICOGRAPHER

Side 1

Vocabulary Develop First 2 columns are to be done <u>DURING</u> READING,
then the **rest is completed during your job time.**

Student's Name: _Michael_   Book Title: _Harriet Tubman Freedom Leader_

<u>LEXICOGRAPHER</u>: Your job is to create a vocabulary dictionary while reading. Write the
PAGE, PARAGRAPH, & WORD(s) that you or your group finds challenging, thought
provoking, puzzling, or unfamiliar while reading. During job time, you will look them up in a
dictionary & thesaurus (use computer website, if available) and **complete the chart for EACH
day.** If you cannot find a synonym or antonym, your team should help you WITH clues from
the definition or context clues. During sharing time, DISCUSS your information rather than
merely reading from this sheet.

On the chart **Pg / P = Page / Paragraph #**
Be sure the definition fits the word in the story context.

TODAY'S Date: _5-5-09_ READ from page _70_ to _91_ DATE SHARED: _5-6-09_ Super! +20

Pg /P	WORD	DICTIONARY DEFINITION that Fits the CONTEXT	Part of Speech	SYNONYM	ANTONYM
70/1	hearse	vehicle used for carrying the dead	N	None	None
7/1	exhaustion	being very tired	N	wiped out	Hyper
78/3	shrugged	a gesture showing a lack concern	V	moved shoulder updown	None
83/3	brutally	violent	adj\adv	cruel	Kind
87/5	desperately	reckless / lost hope	adj\adv	hopeless	hopeful

TODAY'S Date: _5-6-09_ READ from page _92_ to _115_ DATE SHARED: _5-7-09_ excellent work! +20

Pg /P	WORD	DICTIONARY DEFINITION that Fits the CONTEXT	Part of Speech	SYNONYM	ANTONYM
94/3	reluctant	un willing	Adj	hesistant	eager
97/2	gun boats	small armed a ship that cant move in shallow water	N	None	None
100/5	scattered	separate, to go in different directo	V	tossing around	gather
113/1	tenderly	Needing careful handing	adj\adv	sensitive	uncaring
114/4	Indigent	poor , needy	adj\n	needy	rich

See BACK SIDE for the NEXT 3 days ⟹

LITERARY ENLIGHTENER'S Name: _Tevelisse R._ Side 2

❖Suggestions for choosing each selection:
  ❑ FIGURATIVE LANGUAGE: simile, metaphor, onomatopoeia , idiom
  ❑ MOOD: humorous, sad, frightening, suspenseful, mysterious
  ❑ TONE: author's attitude or opinion through words or actions of characters
  ❑ THOUGHT-PROVOKING: the lines encourage higher-level thinking
  ❑ ANALYZING WORDS in TEXT: giving the text meaning beyond what it tells you directly
  ❑ IMAGERY: text that create a visual imagine

TODAY'S Date: _4/30_ READ from page _38_ to _48_ DATE SHARED: _5/1_
Selection: Page #: _48_ Paragraph #: _4_ Suggestion you chose: _____
Words from the text: _Tears filled Harriets eyes as she_
stepped slowly across the line. _+20 Very_
insightful!

Explain why you selected this section. _I choose this passage because the_
tone shows that Harriet was emotional as she reached the line because
the very thing she had wanted "Freedom" was already in the palm of her hand.

TODAY'S Date: _5/4_ READ from page _49_ to _69_ DATE SHARED: _5/5_
Selection: Page #: _58_ Paragraph #: _5_ Suggestion you chose: _____
Words from the text: _"They won't ever catch me. I know in my_
soul that they won't, Never!"
_+20_

Explain why you selected this section. _I choose this passage because the mood_
the author uses for Harriet is strong and determind. It shows that
Harriet will not let anyone or anything get in the way of her
dream, to be free and to help other slaves be free too.

TODAY'S Date: _5/5_ READ from page _70_ to _82_ DATE SHARED: _5/6_
Selection: Page #: _88_ Paragraph #: _2_ Suggestion you chose: _____
Words from the text: _"I won't have done all I can do until_
the war is over and every slave is free." _+20_ _Love your comments!_

Explain why you selected this section. _I selected this passage because one_
tone shows that even though the U.S is fighting to end slavery
and Harriet has freed many she still wants to help slaves no matter
what the condition is.

SKILLS: Figurative Language; Mood; Tone; Analyzing Text; Imagery

Literature Circles: The Reading Buddies © 2009

85

LITERARY LOCKSMITH...Unlocking the Character   Side 1

To be done **AFTER** READING, **NOT** while you are reading.

Student's Name: *Molly*   Book Title: Harriet Tubman: Freedom leader

LITERARY LOCKSMITH: Your job is to select a character EACH day & "unlock" information about the Character so that your group has a key to better understand this character.

Examples of Character TRAITS : kind, unkind, ambitious, lazy, brave, courageous, determined, powerful, obedient, rebellious, leader, follower, strong, weak

Examples of FEELINGS (emotions or moods): love, affection, anger, guilt, depression, fear, joy, delight, frustration

TODAY'S Date: 4-28-9 READ from page 1 to 24 DATE SHARED: 4-29-09

Character's Name Harriet

The Character's **TRAITS**:
Harriet is determind, very rebellious, and strong.

FEELINGS experienced by this Character: Anger and Hope
WHY did he/she feel this way?
She felt anger towards her masters, but also hope for slaves to become free

+20 Well done!

EXPLAIN how YOU FEEL about this Character.
I feel that Harriet Tubman is very strong and rebellious and wants to fight to become free.

TODAY'S Date: 4-29-09 Read from page 24 to 38 DATE SHARED: _____   *-1*
+19

Character's Name John

The Character's **TRAITS**:
John was mean, unfaithful, and carefree, lazy.

FEELINGS experienced by this Character: annoyed
WHY did he/she feel this way?
He got annoyed whenever Harriet talked about becoming free.

EXPLAIN how YOU FEEL about this Character.
I feel that John was very annoying himself and takes advantage of Harriet.

See BACK SIDE for the NEXT 3 days ➡

PLOT PREDICTOR

Side 1

To be done **AFTER** READING, **NOT while you are reading**.

Student's Name: Jessica Book Title: Harriet Tubman: Freedom Leader

PLOT PREDICTOR: Your job is to predict what you think will happen after reading EACH day. **On Day 2-5** of your job, **you will respond to your predictions from the previous day BEFORE** you make another prediction. You will share during discussion time.

+20

Great predictions

TODAY'S Date: 4-28 READ from page 1 to 24 DATE SHARED: 4-29

What do you think will happen next? List different possible outcomes.	What is the basis for your predictions? (Why did you make these predictions?)
Harriet + Jim will try + escape to the underground rail road. Another outcome can be is that Harriet + Jim try to escape but they get caught and the kill Jim but Harriet manages to escape.	The basics for my prediction is escape because that is what Harriet thinks and wants to do. Plus with the information that Jim gave her she knows about the underground rail road.

TODAY'S Date: 4-29 READ from page 24 to 39 DATE SHARED: 4-30

Use examples from the text to explain how yesterday's predictions were CONFIRMED or CONFIRMED.	What do you think will happen next? List different possible outcomes.	What is the basis for your predictions? Why did you make these predictions?)
Harrit and Jim both tried to escape to the under ground railroad. Harriet didn't get caught. +20	Harriet will continue the trail By herself because her brothers are to scared to continue along the way they all get caught but only Harriet manages to escape.	because her brothers are scared and are thinking that they don't want to go on because the slave catchers will be looking for them. !!

Wonderful confirmation!

Very detailed!!

See BACK SIDE for the NEXT 3 days →

SKILL: Making Predictions; Drawing:

Literature Circles The Reading Buddies © 2009

STORY CARTOGRAPHER

Side 1

Story Map for 5-Day Cycle

To be done __AFTER__ READING, __NOT__ while you are reading.

Student's Name: _Petra_   Book Title: _Harriet Tubman: Freedom leader_

__STORY CARTOGRAPHER__: A cartographer creates maps. Your job is to create a STORY MAP about what you've read. There may not be a solution/outcome each day. You will share your story map during your group's discussion time.

TODAY'S Date: _5/6_   READ from page _92_ to _119_ DATE SHARED: _5-7_

Setting (Where & when): november 1862	Important Event 1: Harriet gladly took of the job of a spy	Solution/Outcome The union soliders were able to defeat the rebels; that was a great help towards the war
Main Characters: Harriet	Important Event 2: Harriet in her union outfit went to a Plantation told the slaves they were Free! get information	
Plot (Problem-Situation): Harriet is to be a spy, and also inform slaves of their Freedom.	Important Event 3: Harriet got the information on the rebels camp, and were there ammunition was located	

+20 Very thorough story elements!

TODAY'S Date: _____   READ from page _____ to _____ DATE SHARED: _____

Setting (Where & when):	Important Event 1:	Solution/Outcome
Main Characters:	Important Event 2:	
Plot (Problem-Situation):	Important Event 3:	

See BACK SIDE for the NEXT 3 days ⟶

Skill: Story Elements; Plot Development; Main Idea; Details; Conflict/Resolution

Literature Circles: The Reading Buddies © 2009

88

STORY RECAPITULATOR

Side 1

Brief Summary

Student's Name: _Shannon   C_   Book Title: _Payback_ _100% awesome_

To be done **AFTER** READING, **NOT** while you are reading.

<u>RECAPITULATOR</u>: You will write a **brief SUMMARY (recap)** of what the group reads **EACH day**. It should focus on the highlights or **important ideas** of what you read, including the **key events**. You will share your summary during your group's discussion time.

TODAY'S Date: _12-1_ . READ from **page** _1_ to _10½_ DATE SHARED: _12-2_

Write your **summary (recap)** of today's reading: _Tyray got in trouble because he got in a fight with Darrel and Tyray broke his wrist then he got suspended for three days. Next the dad started yelling and hitting Tyray and busted his lip. Dad threatened Tyray that if he gets in anymore trouble in the next three days, he is going to break his other wrist. We learned that Tyray's brother went to jail for armed robbery and found out that Tyray father is also a bully._ _Excellent summary +20_

TODAY'S Date: _12-2_ READ from **page** _11_ to _19_ DATE SHARED: _NS_

Write your **summary (recap)** of today's reading: _Tyray finally went back to school after the three days and everybody was acting different. When tyray was going to class this girl named Lark started talking to him and said "I'm sorry about your wrist". All of a sudden they started hanging out. When Tyray was in the cafeteria he had some flash backs about what happened and he kept saying in his head just wait because he wants to get revenge and he did not to look at that spot where the accident happened._ _You do a very thorough job! +20_

See BACK SIDE for the NEXT 3 days ➡

SKILL: Comprehension; Main Idea; Details; Summarizing Key Events

89   Literature Circles: The Reading Buddies © 2009

TEXT CONNECTOR   Side 1

Student's Name: _Patricia_____   Book Title: _Harriet Tubman Freedom_
                                                                Leader

TEXT CONNECTOR: Your job is to make **one** interesting **connection**, EACH DAY, between your reading (text) & the world beyond the book. You will explain how the characters, setting, or events in the TEXT relate (connect) to one of these choices:

- ❑ to **SELF** (your life, your friends),
- ❑ to **WORLD** (other people, problems, events),
- ❑ to **TEXT** (another book or story that you've read).

Be **specific** & **thorough** so that we understand the **reason** for your connection.

CIRCLE the type of connection you make each day, & use complete sentences.

TODAY'S Date: _4-29-09_ READ from page _1_ to _24_ DATE SHARED: _4-30-09_

CONNECTION: (CIRCLE) the connection you made: TEXT to [SELF, (WORLD), TEXT]   +18

it reminded me of
When Harriet stole from Miss Sarah. When my cousin was smaller and stole from his Mom when we were eating at a restaurant. And then she put the money on the table. and when nobody was "looking my cousin grabbed the money and put it in his pocket.

(left margin, handwritten) – I see my grammar corrections. Use complete sentences. ☺

TODAY'S Date: _____   READ from page _24_ to _38_ DATE SHARED: _____   +9

CONNECTION: (CIRCLE) the connection you made: TEXT to [SELF, WORLD... TEXT]
The next day, Jim was strangely silent all morning. He knew he was going to do someting so he acted kind of different. Like nervous and impatient. –9

(handwritten in cursive) Patricia ~ what happened? You need to explain the connection

(handwritten) See me before moving on ☺

See BACK SIDE for the NEXT 3 days ⟶

CHARACTER COMPARISONS ~~ END OF BOOK ASSESSMENT

Name: Elizabeth   Date: 5/7   Period: 1

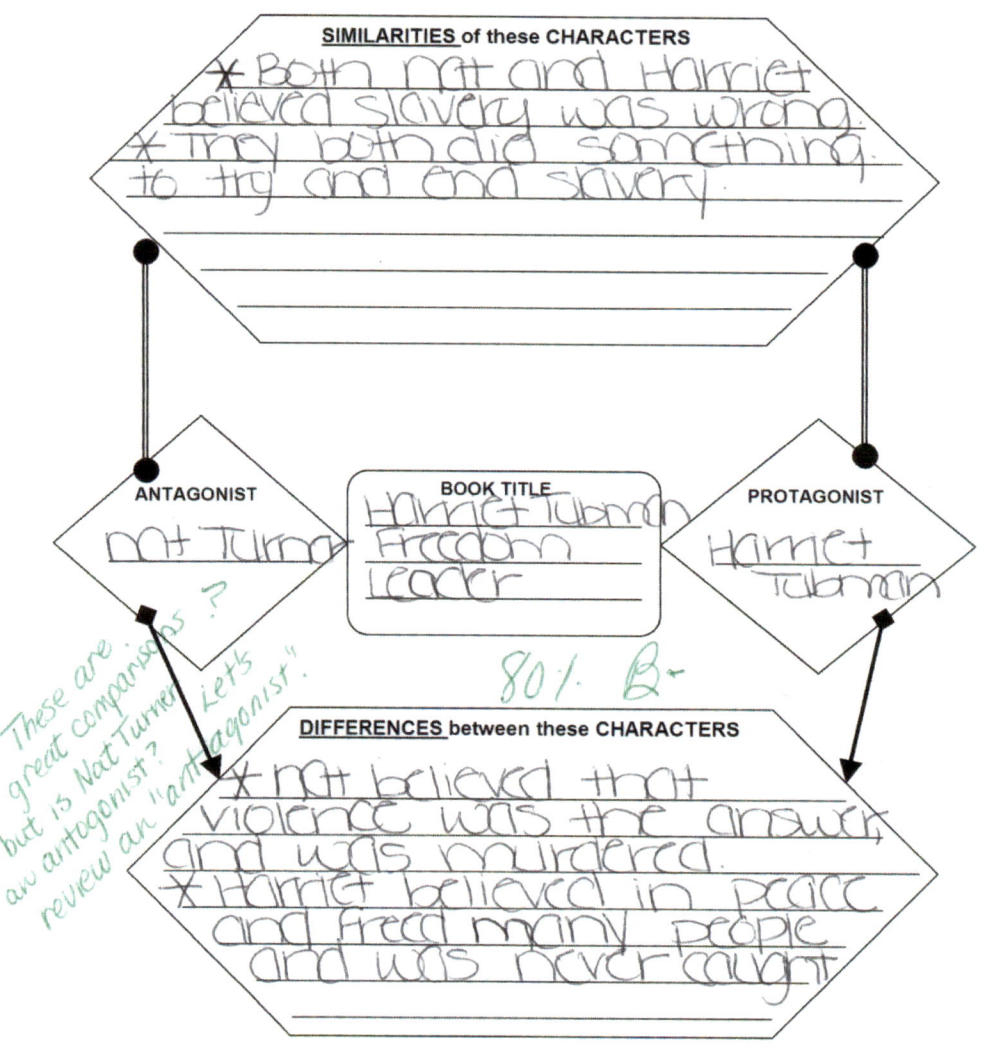

SIMILARITIES of these CHARACTERS

✗ Both Nat and Harriet
believed slavery was wrong.
✗ They both did something
to try and end slavery.

ANTAGONIST

Nat Turner

BOOK TITLE

Harriet Tubman
Freedom
Leader

PROTAGONIST

Harriet
Tubman

These are
great comparisons ?
but is Nat Turner Lets
an antagonist? review an "antagonist".

80% B-

DIFFERENCES between these CHARACTERS

✗ Nat believed that
violence was the answer
and was murdered.
✗ Harriet believed in peace
and freed many people
and was never caught

SKILLS: Character Development; Compare & Contrast   Literature Circles: The Reading Buddies © 2009

91

USER RESPONSES to Literature Circles

I really enjoyed the literature circle. I felt it was a very resourceful way of reading a book. I would highly enjoy doing it again in high school. I also enjoyed the jobs, which allowed us to recount what we enjoyed the most. Thank you for giving us this experience.
Caroline ~ 8th grade

The literacy circle was a good experience for me. When we can read together it's a good way to make sure everybody understands the book. Also, some of the book choices were books that I would never think of reading.
Amanda ~ 8th grade

The (small group) literature circle was very fun. I enjoyed being able to work with my friends and enjoy the book together. I also enjoyed the books we chose.
Robert ~ 8th grade

I thought the literature circle was helpful because we learned different sides and details from other people and that we got to read as a class. You could improve it by doing it more often.
Adrian ~ 8th grade

I enjoyed the literature circle because you can talk to the whole class in one circle.
People can help you if you need help.
Eileen ~ 8th Grade

I also liked the literature circle because everybody got to read and discuss at the same time. It helped the students to understand about the book.
April ~ 8th Grade

The literature circle was fun because it was something different and gave us more reading experience. It's harder reading out loud. I don't know why, but for some reason I loved reading in class 'cause I rarely read at home. Reading in class got me reading at home more.
Francee ~ 8th Grade

The things I liked about literature circles were reading out loud, each person expressing their own opinion about the book, and the jobs were helpful in comprehending what we read.
Ashley ~ 7th Grade

I think doing a literature circle was a fun experience. I liked working in groups. The jobs were helpful because they made it so much easier to remember what's going on in the book.
Megan ~ Grade 7

I liked how we sat in a circle. It was easier to see people read and share jobs. I also liked the "Success of the Circle"—the way we showed how to be respectful in the circle. The jobs were helpful to learn how to do different skills: cause and effect, predicting what would happen next, and learning the traits of different characters.
Kya ~ Grade 7

USER RESPONSES to Literature Circles continued

Doing literature circles is a great way for kids to learn and it encourages us to read books. The jobs were helpful because they kept me on track. I never knew I could be so into a book!
Shannon ~ Grade 8

We all had a chance to read and it helped us with our reading and communication skills. The jobs helped us understand the story more and actually think about the book. It was excellent.
Jehiel ~ Grade 8

I loved being able to share our opinions, read, and it helped us with our reading skills. The jobs helped us to remember and understand the story.
Yarlety ~ Grade 7

During its' development, I experienced using <u>Literature Circles: A Ready… Set…Teach Literature Circle Program for All Content Areas Grades 6-12</u> as a substitute teacher. I instructed Developmental and Intensive Reading classes with the materials for an entire week. Although I am not a reading teacher, and the materials were novel to me, we had an excellently productive week.

<u>Literature Circles: A Ready… Set…Teach Literature Circle Program for All Content Areas Grades 6-12</u> provides an organized format and logical flow of activities for maximizing comprehension. With student job responsibilities specified (i.e. Text Connector, Didactic Detective, Elemental Artist, Literary Locksmith, and Story Recapitulator), adequate time for reading and reporting allowed, and self-directed recording sheets provided, the class work routine was readily established.

Students were receptive and responsive to the overall structure of literature circle time. They understood the importance of the detailed directions and their accountability for each job responsibility. They appreciated the expectation that they concentrate on the single, assigned job. Students were anxious to hear interpretations from the other assignments. For me, the commanding elements of these materials are their thoroughness and adaptability. They qualify as truly "user friendly" for teachers and students.

Sally J. Stevens
Family & Consumer Science Educator
Substitute Teacher, Lee County, Florida